The World of Unseen Spirits

A Study Guide / Bernard N. Schneider

The World

of

Unseen Spirits

The World

of

Unseen Spirits

A Study Guide

By Bernard N. Schneider

BMH BOOKS

WINONA LAKE, INDIANA

ISBN: 0-88469-024-5

COPYRIGHT 1975
BMH BOOKS
WINONA LAKE, INDIANA

PRINTED IN U.S.A.

COVER PHOTO: CHARLES W. TURNER

ACKNOWLEDGMENTS

The author desires to express his sincere appreciation to the following persons for their valuable help in preparing this volume:

To Mrs. Gerda Schnieders who typed the original manuscript as a labor of love.

To Mrs. Betty Church who supplied me with important research material.

And to my wife, Mary E. Schneider, who lovingly applied her background in journalism in making many valuable suggestions to the composition of this book.

DEDICATION

This book is affectionately dedicated to the faithful members of the four congregations whom it was my privilege to serve as pastor over a span of forty years.

Foreword

In recent years the world has had great exposure to the realm of the unseen. Magazines, both secular and sacred, have devoted numerous pages to the area of the occult. Much of the material has laid great stress on false worship and demonism. At BMH Books we felt a desire to approach this subject from a much wider Biblical perspective and also touch on the subject of the spirit world of angels.

Dr. Bernard Schneider, who is presently pastor of the Grace Brethren Bible Church of Fort Myers, Florida, has approached this study guide as he has his teaching ministry—in a practical and understandable manner. He has been known for his ability to take the great truths of the Scripture and bring them into words that can be grasped by his hearers and readers. You will find this true in the material which you are about to study.

He deals with the whole spectrum of the unseen world of spirits, both good and evil. His balanced writing will open to the student a rare opportunity of personal edification as well as words of caution for godly living. Selected Bible readings will aid in your receiving a great blessing from this material.

Dr. Schneider's personal touch shows through this work. In addition to his present pastorate, he has served churches in Washington, D.C.; Covington, Virginia; and Mansfield, Ohio. Through the years of his ministry his Bible teaching has had a human touch. He has spoken to various conferences and has authored materials for Bible study usage. BMH Books is gratified to present *The World of Unseen Spirits* for your spiritual encouragement.

—Charles W. Turner
Executive Editor, BMH Books

Preface

Life is exciting in this Space Age of man's history. To sit in your living room watching men bouncing around on the moon, and listening to their conversations—that is exciting. Reading of a planned round-trip shuttle service from earth to space, knowing that it is not fantasy but just a matter of economics and a little more experimenting, still takes your breath away. The marvelous results of scientific research are made available to man at an ever-accelerating pace, and we are wondering what will be next. It is great to be alive in these days, and I am glad I did not miss them.

The Space Age is also presenting some perplexing paradoxes. With the accent on greater speed and more power, we are suddenly faced with an energy crisis and a revival of the bicycle. Insignificant nations whose names and locations were somewhat nebulous to most of the world are suddenly dictating how the rest of the world shall live. One of the most surprising paradoxes of our time is the phenomenal surge of interest in the realm of spirit-beings. This is taking place in a world which has become so materialistically oriented that any display of interest in life after death is considered a sign of ignorance. This involvement in spirits is more like an epidemic than a fad, and it is finding expression in different forms of experimentation with some tragic results.

A great deal is being written these days about the renewed interest in spirits and about the many different turns that this concern is taking (it seems that not only has man taken a new interest in spirits, but the spirits have taken a new interest in man as well). This book is written mainly to present what God has revealed in His Word about unseen spirits, and what man's attitude should be toward them.

The reality of a great host of unseen spirits who exert tremendous influence in the world of people is certainly not a new discovery. The Word of God vividly describes their origin, character, activity, purpose, and power. Their presence and working are confirmed through experience to those who are actively engaged in the spreading of the Gospel. The writer has been preaching and teaching the Word of God for 40 years. It seems impossible to him that anyone who has devoted his life to leading souls out of darkness and sin into the life and peace of God could doubt the reality of spirits. Spirits will do anything to defeat that endeavor.

I am reminded of something a gold miner said to me in 1934. His son and I had been roommates during seminary days. We were invited to try our luck at gold mining during summer vacation in the mountains of northern California. We did not find enough gold to pay for our board, but we surely toughened our bodies with hard digging and sleeping under the stars. A small stream ran close by our camp, and it was fairly obvious that its bed had been moved by rock slides and other causes over past centuries. When other efforts produced no gold, my friend and I decided to dig a pit straight down to where the stream used to be in hopes of finding some nuggets at the bottom. The old miner, who was a fine Christian, approved the idea and suggested that we would have to go down about 33 feet to reach bedrock. Being a greenhorn, I asked naively: "But how will we know when we reach bedrock?" This drew a roar of laughter from the miner and then the rejoinder: "Don't you worry about that. You will know you are there when the pick bounces back at you." I found out later how right he was. I would say the same thing today to those who doubt the reality of Satan and his confederates. When you get involved in the struggle of bringing men and women into contact with the Living Saviour, you soon know of the opposition of a force known in the Bible as "principalities . . . powers . . . rulers of the darkness of this world . . . [and] spiritual wickedness in high places (Eph. 6:12).

—The author

Table of Contents

CHAPTER ONE

Angels: Who Are They?

THE CHAPTER OUTLINED:

I. The Origin of Angels
   1. Angels are created beings
   2. This creative act of God included . . . Satan
   3. The number of angels is very great

II. The Nature of Angels
   1. Angels are spirits or spiritual beings
   2. Angels are without sex distinction
   3. Angels are deathless
   4. Angels are dynamic in power
   5. Angels are holy
   6. Angels are organized and recognize authority

SUGGESTED BACKGROUND DEVOTIONAL READING

Monday—Christ, Creator of the Angels (Col. 1:12-19)
Tuesday—Christ Worshiped by the Angels (Heb. 1:1-6)
Wednesday—Angels As Serving Spirits (Heb. 1:7-14)
Thursday—We Shall Be Equal to the Angels (Luke 20:27-36)
Friday—"Lord, . . . Open His Eyes" (II Kings 6:14-17)
Saturday—We Should Learn from the Angels (II Peter 2:9-15)
Sunday—Jesus Will Come with Angels (II Thess. 1:7-12)

Angels are spiritual beings existing in a different state of being than that which is known to human experience, and they are part of God's heavenly family. The Word of God does not give us a detailed description of them, but treats their existence as a fact and speaks of them often, mostly incidentally. It is very evident that angels have a large part in God's plan and program for man. From these incidentals we learn a great deal about them. We should always remember that not any part of God's Word is written just to satisfy human curiosity, which fact testifies to its divine inspiration. Nevertheless, we can be assured that God has revealed all about the angels that we need to know.

Is the study of angels of any real practical value to the believer? In answer I cite the fact that the Bible mentions angels at least 273 times, and three fifths of these references are found in the New Testament. Since we are told that "all scripture is given by inspiration of God, and is profitable," and since the angels are all "sent forth to minister for them who shall be heirs of salvation," it should be of great practical value to study more closely these servants of God who so often seem to dispense the providences of God. Isn't it interesting to find our Lord Jesus telling us that in the next world we shall be "as the angels of God in heaven"? (Matt. 22:30). Our hearts will be filled with praise to God when we know more of the greatness of His wisdom and power as demonstrated in His gracious provision for us. This gracious provision includes the angels.

At this juncture I want to call attention to a curious situation existing in the world today. While preparing to write this study guide, I tried to secure as much as possible on the subject of spirits. Of course, I soon discovered that the market is literally flooded with recent books, pamphlets, magazine and newspaper articles on the general subject of spirits. However, almost all the published material deals with adverse or evil spirits. Very little is said about the good spirits who are far more numerous and far more important to the well-being of mankind than are the evil or adverse spirits. This peculiar fact has its parallel in the news to which we are exposed day after day. It seems that the only news worth telling these days is bad news which takes up 90 percent of the time and space given to news, both on television and in the newspapers. Could there possibly be a significant relationship between these two parallels? Could there be an unseen pressure from the "god of this world" which influences the choice of subject matter to be published, both orally and in printed form? After all, that which is published greatly shapes the thinking of man. At any rate, let us find out all we can about the angels, the good spirits, and about their activities.

In the Old Testament Hebrew language the word for angel is *malak,* while in the New Testament Greek it is *aggelos.* When translated, both words mean "messenger." The holy angels are messengers of God who carry out His will. There are fallen angels who are evil. They carry out Satan's will where possible. In this chapter we shall limit our study mainly to the holy angels of God and will divide the subject as follows:

> The Origin of Angels, or Where Did They Come From?
> The Nature of Angels, or What Are They Like?

I. The Origin of Angels

Have angels always existed? Are they eternal, like God? The answer is that they are not eternal, but had a beginning somewhere in time. How long ago they came into being we are not told, but the Scriptures indicate that they were already present when the Lord created the earth (cf. Job 38:7). The following facts about their origin can be found in the Word of God:

1. Angels are created beings. Speaking of the deity of Christ, the Holy Spirit tells us: "For by him were all things created, that are in heaven, and that are in earth, visible and invisible, whether they be thrones, or dominions, or principalities, or powers: all things were created by him, and for him" (Col. 1:16). The "invisible" things in heaven were created by the Son of God. This certainly includes the angels. The thrones and dominions, principalities and powers are representative of the different ranks and functions of the angels. The Twentieth Century Translation renders this: "Angels and archangels, and all the powers of heaven."

2. This creative act of God included the fallen angels, even Satan. The Bible makes it very clear that the devil was created a perfect being who at a later date rebelled against God. Referring to Satan, one Scripture verse says: "Thou wast perfect in thy ways from the day that thou wast created, *till* iniquity was found in thee" (Ezek. 28:15). The context of this revealing statement will be considered in a later chapter on the personality of Satan. At this point our attention is attracted to three facts, namely: (1) The highest of all the angels was *created.* (2) He was *perfect* when he was created. (3) At a later time he changed, became evil, as indicated by the phrase: "*till* iniquity was found in thee."

3. The number of angels is very great. How many angels are there? A hundred thousand? A thousand thousand? Their number is far greater than that. We all remember what Jesus said to Peter when that impulsive disciple grabbed a sword and started to fight the officers sent out to arrest Jesus. "Thinkest thou that I cannot now pray to my Father, and he shall presently give me more than twelve legions of angels? But how then shall the scriptures be fulfilled, that thus it must be?" (Matt. 26:53-54). A legion was a Roman army of from 6,000 to 10,000 men. So Jesus was talking of about 72,000 angels, any one of whom would have been of more use than Peter.

The Bible tells us: "But ye are come to mount Sion, and unto the city of the living God, the heavenly Jerusalem, and to an *innumerable company* of angels" (Heb. 12:22). "Countless multitudes of angels" would be a good translation of this verse. We do not know how many it takes to make a countless multitude. Our horizons are somewhat widened, however, when in another place we read that 100 million angels are present, plus thousands of thousands more, when the Lord opens the book with the seven seals preparatory to His coming again in glory (cf. Rev. 5:11). Quite naturally we are taken up with the number and accomplishments of the human family. When we shall enter that other world of beings, unseen to us now, we may well discover that the family of God in heaven is far greater in number and in accomplishments than the human family. There is no "Angel Crisis" in heaven!

II. The Nature of Angels

The nature and attributes of angels cover a wide range of study involving many verses of Scripture. We will consider the most important aspects.

1. Angels are spirits or spiritual beings. "And of the angels he saith, Who maketh his angels spirits . . ." (Heb. 1:7). "Are they not all ministering spirits . . .?" (Heb. 1:14). Few if any Bible words are as difficult to define as is the word "spirit." Jesus declared that "God is . . . spirit: and they that worship him must worship him in spirit and in truth" (John 4:24).

The basic idea from which the word "spirit" is derived is that of air or wind. Air is very real but not visible to the natural eye. Spirits are real and intelligent beings who are not normally visible to the human eye because they do not have a natural body. For the same reason they are not subject to the natural or physical laws of the universe. This permits them to move from place to place just like our minds can move from place to place in the twinkling of an eye. Man, too, has a spirit, but while alive physically, his spirit is confined to his body, and this physical body is bound to the laws of nature. When moving from place to place man now has to move the whole distance physically, even when he avails himself of jet or rocket power to speed up the motion. Man's present body is created for life only on this earth. He has to breathe, eat, and drink to live. If he leaves this earth physically, he has to take part of the earth with him to keep alive—including food, drink and atmosphere. A spirit obviously does not need any of these things. Spirits can live, move and operate anywhere in the universe. This is a difference too great for us to fully understand or appreciate. But when we shall receive our glorified bodies, we, too, will be free from the limitations of earth-life.

What about angels in human form? In the records of God's Word angels often appear in the likeness of human beings with bodies that could be seen by human eyes. This was apparently a special manifestation arranged for the benefit of those people to whom the angels were sent. Whether those bodies were real or only appeared so, we cannot say dogmatically, because we are not told. However, we are told that on occasion these angels in human form partook of food and drink. The Lord with two angels visited Abraham and Sarah, and the three guests were entertained with all the courtesy at Abraham's command. We are told that when a meal was hastily prepared and served under the trees, "they did eat" (Gen. 18:8). Apparently that same evening the two angels came to Lot at the gate of Sodom. At Lot's insistence they went home with him, and there "he made them a feast, and did bake unleavened bread, and they did eat" (Gen. 19:3). A very interesting passage in which believers are exhorted to practice Christian hospitality, states that by entertaining strangers, "some have entertained angels unawares" (Heb. 13:2).

Sometimes angels appearing in human form suddenly disappeared, as in the case of Peter's deliverance from prison (cf. Acts 12:6-10). This does not prove that the bodies were unreal, for our Lord in His resurrection body suddenly appeared in a room, even ate with His disciples, and just as suddenly disappeared (cf. Luke 24:30-43). There certainly was no question about the reality of His body. Just because a body cannot be seen by our natural sight, except by special enablement, does not necessarily mean that the body is not real. It does mean that such is not a natural body.

However, just as there is a natural body, so is there also a "spiritual body" (I Cor. 15:44). At the second coming of Christ believers too shall receive their spiritual bodies, and then we shall be "as the angels of God in heaven" (Matt. 22:30). We are assured in the Word of God that there are "celestial bodies, and bodies terrestrial" (I Cor. 15:40).

2. **Angels are without sex distinction.** Wherever angels appear in human form in the Bible, they are presented in the masculine gender and never spoken of as being female. The angels who appeared to Abraham are spoken of as "men" (Gen. 19:2, 5-11). The angel who wrestled with Jacob is called "a man" (Gen. 32:24).

On that glad Easter morning when the women found the grave empty, there suddenly stood by them "two men . . . in shining garments" (Luke 24:4). These "men" were angels. At the Ascension, forty days later, when the faithful stood gazing toward heaven where Jesus had disappeared behind a cloud, "two men stood by them in white apparel" (Acts 1:10). They also were angels from heaven. The Greek word in these verses which is translated "men," is *andres,* which is a nominative plural of *aner.* The *Analytical Greek Lexicon* defines this as "a male person of full age and stature, as opposed to a child or a female."

Our Lord provided some light on the question of angels and their sex when He answered the Sadducees who were trying to embarrass Him with a question about the resurrection. Jesus stated that in the resurrection people will neither marry nor be given in marriage, but will be equal to the angels (cf. Luke 20:27-36). Obviously this means that sex will have no part in the life to come, but we will be equal to, or like the angels, with the strong implication that angels have no sex life either.

The plan of God for this world whereby the human race is secured calls for propagation. For that purpose there is born within all physical life the sex urge and the desire to produce one's own kind. But angels are different. Sex is strictly an earthly function and there is no counterpart in heaven.

3. **Angels are deathless.** Jesus said of the resurrected saints: "Neither can they die any more: for they are equal unto the angels" (Luke 20:36). Angels never increase or decrease in number. There is no propagation and no death. As far as we know, of all the family of God made up of intelligent, morally free, and therefore responsible beings, only man is subject to physical death. This is one reason why the Son of God did not take upon himself the nature of angels when He came to redeem man from sin, for

angels cannot die (cf. Heb. 2:9-16).

4. Angels are dynamic in power. They are called "mighty angels" (II Thess. 1:7). The Greek word for mighty in this instance is *dunameos,* coming from *dunamis,* from which we get our words such as dynamite, dynamic, and so forth. The angels are full of strength. Their might and strength is mentioned repeatedly in the Bible. The Psalmist sang: "Bless the Lord, ye his angels, that excel in strength" (Ps. 103:20). Angels are mightier in power than human rulers or government (II Peter 2:10-11).

When those faithful women walked to the grave where Jesus had been buried three days earlier, intending to properly annoint His body, they said to each other: "Who shall roll us away the stone from the door of the sepulchre?" (Mark 16:3). The next verse tells us that the stone was "very great." But the problem had been solved by one of the mighty angels: "And, behold, there was a great earthquake: for an angel of the Lord descended from heaven, and came and rolled back the stone from the door, and sat upon it. His countenance was like lightning, and his raiment white as snow" (Matt. 28:2-3). Commissioned by God, angels have power to destroy cities (cf. Gen. 19:12-13); put a strong army to death (cf. II Kings 19:35); smite wicked men with blindness (cf. Gen. 19:10-11); untie a chained prisoner and lead him out of a locked and well-guarded cell without awakening the guards (cf. Acts 12:7-11). Angels have power to shut the mouths of hungry lions (cf. Dan. 6:21-22). By their superior understanding of all the workings of nature, they can do greater things than even modern man is able to accomplish in his ever-widening under-standing of these same workings. Thus angels are able to carry out any assignment God gives to them.

It should be noted here that although angels have superior power, they do not have unlimited power. They cannot create. They cannot bring forth without preexisting material. Only God can create without any material on hand. It is evident that angels use their power only in carrying out God's will, for they "do his commandments, harkening unto the voice of his word" (Ps. 103:20).

5. Angels are holy. God's Word assures us that the angels are holy. Jesus said: "When the Son of man shall come in his glory, and all the holy angels with him" (Matt. 25:31; cf. Mark 8:38 and Rev. 14:10).

From the entire Biblical record concerning angels we are led to believe that somewhere back in time angels were tested and took their stand for or against God. While some angels joined Lucifer's rebellion, most chose to be true to God. Due to this test and choice their character was fixed and God's angels are forever loyal and devoted to Him. They are holy, which means they are completely separate from evil and fully devoted to God. As the saved, who have made their choice of God in this life, will be completely separate from sin and temptation in the life to come, so the angels who made their choice of God are without sin or temptation forever. The plain, scriptural picture is that whatever pleases God, makes the angels happy, too.

6. Angels are organized and recognize authority. "God is not the author of confusion, but of peace" (I Cor. 14:33). He commands that "all things be done decently and in order" (v. 40). We are not surprised therefore that such order is found in the organization of His angels. There is Michael who appears to be the designated leader of the angels. He is mentioned by name five times and is called the "archangel" in Jude 9. The title "archangel" simply means the chief angel. The reference to Michael by Jude is an eye-opener. Satan was trying to disturb the body of Moses whom God himself had buried. Michael opposed him, but recognizing the higher office or rank Satan had held in his original creation, the Archangel simply turned the matter over to the Lord. The reason this affair in the spirit world is told by Jude is to emphasize the will of God for people in general, and for believers in particular. Christians are to show respect for rightful authority. Even the angels do.

Here we find the curtain that hides from us the world of spirits is lifted for an instant. Thereby, we get a glimpse of the tremendous conflicts and activities that take place in the world that now is unseen to man. But if wars are fought over the corpse of a man, what conflicts must rage over the souls of men and women for whom Christ died! No wonder there is rejoicing in heaven in the presence of the angels over one sinner that repents!

Another indication of Michael's leadership is found in the Book of the Revelation where we read: "And there was war in heaven: Michael and his angels fought against the dragon; and the dragon fought and his angels, and prevailed not . . ." (Rev. 12:7-8). The "dragon" is Satan as explained in verse 9. Michael has his angels over which he rules under the direction of God. According to Daniel 12:1, Michael is especially appointed to stand up for the Children of Israel in the days of the Great Tribulation.

Gabriel is another angel of superior rank, judging from the commissions assigned to him by God. We first meet him as a messenger sent to Daniel to explain the meaning of a vision and to give that prophet the famous prediction of the Seventy Weeks (cf. Dan. 8:16; 9:21-27). In the New Testament we find him employed as the messenger who announced the birth of the Forerunner of Christ. We are also told of Gabriel's coming to Mary with the news that she would become the mother of the Messiah (cf. Luke 1:11-20, 26-37). The angel introduced himself to Zachariah with: "I am Gabriel, that stand in the presence of God; and am sent to speak unto thee, and to shew thee these glad tidings." Nothing else is told us about Gabriel, whose name means the mighty one of God, or the hero of God. We understand that he is a special messenger of God, entrusted with the most important personal messages of God to men and women on earth.

In God's order of heavenly beings there are also cherubims and seraphims. At no time are they presented as angels. Cherubims are mentioned often in the Bible. Seraphims are mentioned only once, and that is in the record of Isaiah's vision of the holiness of God (cf. Isa. 6:1-7). Cherubims are first mentioned in connection with the expulsion of man from the Garden of Eden when God placed cherubims on the east side to guard the way to the Tree of Life (cf. Gen. 3:24). They are closely associated with the throne of God and seem to be guardians of that throne. Of special interest is the indication that Satan was originally of the heavenly clan of cherubims. God's own description of Satan states: "Thou art the anointed cherub that covereth; and I have set thee so" (Ezek. 28:14). Cherub is the singular of cherubim. Satan was anointed of God to be the protector of the very throne of God. How interesting! How shocking!!

A close study of God's Word also points to the probability that the four living creatures of the Book of the Revelation (improperly called "beasts" in the King James translation) are members of the cherubim clan (cf. Ezek. 10:14-15 with Rev. 4:6-8). Another fact worth mentioning is that cherubims and seraphims are presented as having wings. Nowhere in the Bible are angels said to have wings. And there is no reason to believe they are supplied with wings—regardless of the many pictures and sculptures which we have seen of them as winged creatures.

PRACTICAL APPLICATIONS TO THIS CHAPTER

1. The study of the angels fills us with a new wonder at the greatness of God. When we see how mighty the angels are and then realize that they are but creatures of God who constantly worship Him and do His bidding, we may well have a new idea of the majesty of our God.

2. Our hearts are stirred with a new sense of humility as we behold the angels eagerly carrying out God's will. It will keep us from becoming proud of our service if we consider the perfect service of the angels.

3. We should be filled with humble gratitude as we consider the fact that God's angels are around us continually, ministering to us in many ways—ways of which we are not aware. Angels are part of God's loving providence over us.

4. The study of angels fills us with a new wonder at the love of God for man. The redeemed from among mankind will constitute the Bride of Christ, instead of the angels. No wonder the angels desire to look into this mystery of God's love!

CHAPTER TWO

Jesus Christ and the Angels

THE CHAPTER OUTLINED:

I. Angels Announced Christ's Birth into the Human Family
1. The birth of the Forerunner
2. Gabriel announced the conception of Jesus to the Virgin Mary
3. Joseph advised by an angel
4. Angels were present when Jesus was born in Bethlehem
5. An angel directed the child's flight into Egypt
6. The angel called on Joseph in Egypt

II. The Ministry of Angels at the Temptation of Christ

III. Christ Was Strengthened by an Angel in Gethsemane

IV. Angels Were Present at Christ's Resurrection
1. An angel rolled away the stone from the grave
2. An angel told the women to inform the disciples of the resurrection

V. Angels Were Present at the Ascension of Christ

VI. The Angels Will Be Very Active when Christ Returns
1. The Archangel will be heard at the resurrection and the rapture
2. The elect of Israel will be especially protected by the angels
3. Angels will carry out various judgments of God in the Last Day
4. Holy angels will engage in a great warfare with Satan and his angels
5. All the holy angels will accompany Christ when He returns in glory
6. An angel will arrest and imprison Satan for a thousand years

SUGGESTED BACKGROUND DEVOTIONAL READING

Monday—Christ Made Lower than Angels (Heb. 2:1-9)

Tuesday—Christ Made Perfect through Sufferings (Heb. 2:10-18)

Wednesday—Stricken Dumb Because of Unbelief (Luke 1:13-22)

Thursday—The Beautiful Faith of Mary (Luke 1:26-38)

Friday—"Angels . . . Ministered Unto Him" (Matt. 4:1-11)

Saturday—Strengthened by an Angel (Luke 22:39-46)

Sunday—A Special Message from Angels (Acts 1:9-14)

"But we see Jesus, who was made a little lower than the angels for the suffering of death, crowned with glory and honour; that he by the grace of God should taste death for every man" (Heb. 2:9).

Through ages past angels had marveled at the wisdom and power of the Son of God in His creation and operation of the universe. They had seen His glory and had praised and adored Him. They had been present when He spoke the world into being. They watched with wonder when He formed man from the dust of the ground and breathed into him the breath of life. They had long witnessed the grief and sorrow of God at the rebellion of man and had been amazed at His patience and long-suffering. Eagerly they had carried out His assignments for them. What a shock it must have been to the angels, what a gasp of wonder must have filled heaven, when one day the announcement came over the heavenly intercom, that the Son of God was about to take upon himself the nature, form, and life experience of man and was actually to become a human being! He who had created the angels, was to become lower than the angels!

It is little wonder, therefore, that even the reserved language of the Gospels is filled with eloquent reports of angelic activities in behalf of Christ during His earthly sojourn in the flesh. We may rest assured that they were always near Him to do His bidding. Now and then they were called upon to assist Him. But though 12 legions stood ready to defend Him, He would not be diverted from His great mission of bringing man back to God by taking our place of sin on Calvary. The Bible indicates that of all the surprises of the angels through the ages, their greatest amazement came when God made possible the salvation of sinful man through the substitutionary death of His Son. We read that "the angels desire to look into" this manifestation of God's wisdom and grace (cf. I Peter 1:12).

A list of the activities of the angels in behalf of Christ provides us with a most interesting study.

I. Angels Announced Christ's Birth into the Human Family

The last message before the coming of Christ to earth had come from God to man through the prophet Malachi. This was the promise that the Lord would send Elijah before the Day of the Lord (cf. Mal. 4:5-6). About 400 years of silence had passed since that promise had been made. But now "the fulness of time" had come, and the plan of God for man's redemption was about to unfold. In this unfolding the angels of God played a real part.

1. The birth of the Forerunner (Luke 1:5-20). Zacharias the priest and his wife, Elizabeth, had lived long and godly lives. Only one thing had clouded their happiness. They had remained childless, and now the evening of life had come for them. They had accepted their loneliness as the will of God. One morning as Zacharias stood within the Holy Place in the Temple, with the golden censer in his hand, he suddenly became aware of an angelic being standing on the right side of the altar. Zacharias was shaking with fear, but the angel reassured him and told him that a son would be born to him and his wife. This son would be great before the Lord, and would go before the Lord "in the spirit and power of Elias" (Luke 1:17). Zacharias was somewhat doubtful that such an impossible thing should happen to them at their advanced age, and asked for some verification of the promise. The angel then identified himself as "Gabriel, that stand in the presence of the Lord." He said the proof of his promise would be that Zacharias would lose the power of speech until the son would be born (cf. Luke 1:18-20). About 32 years later Jesus said of John the Baptist: "And if ye will receive it" (speaking of the kingdom with himself as the King), "this is Elias, which was for to come" (Matt. 11:14).

2. Gabriel announced the conception of Jesus to the Virgin Mary (Luke 1:26-37). The greatest honor ever bestowed upon a human being was conferred upon Mary. She was chosen of God to give birth to the human life of the Son of God. The announcement of this to Mary was made by Gabriel who was sent by God to Nazareth. But, whereas, the announcement of the Forerunner's birth had been delivered to Zacharias in the Temple, the angel now delivered his message to Mary in the privacy of her home in Nazareth. It was a most unusual salutation with which the angel greeted Mary, and one which certainly bewildered her. "Hail, thou art highly favoured, the Lord is with thee: blessed art thou among women." The angel then unfolded to her the tremendous news that she would become the mother of the Messiah to whom she was to give the name Jesus. He would be called "the Son of the Highest," and He would fulfill the great Davidic hope of a king with an everlasting kingdom.

To Mary's credit it can be said that she did not doubt the news or ask for a sign as Zacharias had done. Though the promise involved an unheard of miracle, the bearing of a child without a human father, Mary in amazing faith responded: "Behold the handmaid of the Lord; be it unto me according to thy word."

3. Joseph advised by an angel (Matt. 1:18-24). Joseph and Mary were engaged to be married. In the Jewish way of life that engagement was as binding as marriage, and it would take a divorce to dissolve it. When Joseph discovered that his bride to be was with child, he was greatly dismayed. He could not marry an unfaithful bride. He did not want to expose her publicly, either. What was he to do? How could he have the contract dissolved privately? As he fell asleep with the problem in his mind, the angel of the Lord appeared to him and informed him of what had really happened to Mary. He was instructed to marry her, for she had been chosen to be the mother of the Messiah. Joseph believed the angel, and he and Mary were married without delay, though they did not live together as husband and wife until after Jesus was born (cf. Matt. 1:24-25).

4. Angels were present when Jesus was born in Bethlehem (Luke 2:8-15). It is understandable that the angels could scarcely contain themselves when Jesus was born that night in a stable near Bethlehem. One of the angels appeared to some shepherds who were awake that night, watching their flocks. The glory of God filled the countryside. Then the angel shouted forth the glad news: "Behold, I bring you good tidings of great joy, which shall be to all people. For unto you is born this day in the city of David a Saviour, which is Christ the Lord" (Luke 2:10-11). And then it happened! As soon as the angel had announced the joyful news, a whole multitude of the angels of heaven united their voices in a mighty chorus of praise and shouted with one accord: "Glory to God in the highest, and on earth peace, good will toward men" (v. 14). A little glimpse behind the curtain is given us by the writer of Hebrews when he tells us of that sacred hour: "And again, when he bringeth in the first begotten into the world, he saith, And let all the angels of God worship him" (Heb. 1:6). It is not at all unreasonable to assume that the angels were present on that night in the stable when their Creator was made flesh and arrived here as a little infant! Of course they worshiped Him!

5. An angel directed the child's flight into Egypt (Matt. 2:13). Cruel, jealous Herod planned to murder the child who was to becomg King of Israel. He was waiting for the Wise Men to return to Jerusalem from Bethlehem where they had gone to worship the newborn King. They were to tell Herod where the baby was to be found. But while Herod waited, the Lord directed the Wise Men to return home another way, and an angel appeared to Joseph, instructing him to take Mary and the baby Jesus and flee into Egypt. They were to remain there until the same angel would send word that it was safe for them to return to their homeland.

6. The angel called on Joseph in Egypt (Matt. 2:19-20). "They are dead which sought the young child's life"—thus the angel informed Joseph. He was directed to return to Israel, and so the little family traveled to Nazareth where they settled down.

II. The Ministry of Angels at the Temptation of Christ

"Then the devil leaveth him, and, behold, angels came and ministered unto him" (Matt. 4:11). Many volumes have been written on the temptation of our Lord, but hardly a line is given to the mission of the angels who came and served Him. But the angels were there. They beheld with holy awe how the Lord of Glory submitted himself to be tried by the cunning snares of Satan. They dared not interfere, but hovered nearby to witness the terrible conflict. And when it was over, when the victory was won in that battle and Christ was left exhausted by the ordeal, the angels were there to minister to His needs, both physical and mental. Exhausted and hungry as He was, the angels refreshed Him with food and with their heavenly company.

III. Christ Was Strengthened by an Angel in Gethsemane

"And there appeared an angel unto him from heaven, strengthening him" (Luke 22:43). Our Lord was in the midst of a crisis so great that we cannot understand its depth. So terrible was the conflict that it brought great drops of blood from His body, which mingled with sweat. As in the wilderness, Satan was present. As in the wilderness, Christ was alone—for the three trusted companions had fallen asleep. Soon He was to drink the bitter cup of the wrath of God upon sin. Then, even God would forsake Him. His soul was filled with agony, and He was utterly lonely. The words: "sorrowful . . . very heavy . . . exceeding sorrowful . . . even unto death" (Matt. 26:37-38), are literally piled on top of each other in the original language to convey the intensity of the agony of soul that He endured. The Greek word for "very heavy" is *ademonein* which literally means "far away from home," or as we would say today: "He was homesick."

It was in the midst of this crisis that an angel came and strengthened Him. The Greek word translated "strengthening" is *enischuo* which is found only twice in the New Testament. It means to give strength or vigor inwardly. Like Elijah who was utterly discouraged and drained of all strength and was revived with food provided by an angel (cf. I Kings 19:5-8); so Jesus was supplied with a source of new strength by an angel that helped to sustain the Lord in the hour of that great crisis.

IV. Angels Were Present at Christ's Resurrection

As we might have expected, the angels played an important role in the triumphs of Christ's resurrection. In fact, they performed a number of different tasks.

1. An angel rolled away the stone from the grave (Matt. 28:1-4). This stone was "very great" (Mark 16:4). We do not believe that the angel rolled away the stone to let Christ out. In His glorified state Christ did not need open doors to pass through. We believe that the sepulchre was opened by the angel in order that the disciples could look in and see that the grave was empty—that Christ was risen.

2. An angel told the women to inform the disciples of the resurrection (Matt. 28:5-8). Mark, who is supposed to have received his information from Peter, tells us that the angel instructed the women: "But go your way, tell his disciples and Peter that he goeth before you into Galilee: there shall ye see him, as he said unto you" (Mark 16:7). A study of all four gospel records indicates that at least two angels remained near the grave that Easter morning to give the glad news of the resurrection to all those who came to visit the grave.

V. Angels Were Present at the Ascension of Christ (Acts 1:10-11)

We can only imagine with what joy the whole host of heaven awaited the return of the Son of God to the Father's house! Though unseen to human eyes, the myriads of angels escorted Him all the way from earth to heaven and worshiped Him as He took His place at the right hand of the Father. However, two of the angels had been appointed to reassure the little band of humans who kept gazing intently into the sky at a spot where a cloud had taken Jesus from their view. These angels are introduced to us as "two men in white apparel." Their task was to tell the faithful followers of Christ that their Lord and Saviour whom they had seen go up into heaven, would some day return just the same way as they had seen Him depart.

It seems significant to me that the last news which the angels were commissioned to bring in connection with the first coming of Christ was a very positive and strong statement to the effect that He would return. When the angels bring us a special message from heaven, we had better believe it. Nothing is more certain to come to pass in the future than the personal, visible return of Christ to this earth.

VI. The Angels Will Be Very Active When Christ Returns

Just as there was a great deal of angelic activity when Christ came the first time, so there will be a tremendous flurry of action among the angels when Christ returns in glory. Jesus constantly associated the angels with His future return in His prophetic utterances. The Book of the Revelation describes the work that angels will perform in the latter days in at least 61 different passages. This number does not include the references to "the angels of the seven churches," found in the first three chapters of the book, nor the several references to the work of fallen angels. The following is a brief and partial outline of angelic activity connected with the second coming of Christ:

1. The Archangel will be heard at the resurrection and the rapture. "For the Lord himself shall descend from heaven with a shout, with the voice of the archangel, and with the trump of God: and the dead in Christ shall rise first: Then we which are alive and remain shall be caught up together with them in the clouds, to meet the Lord in the air: and so shall we ever be with the Lord" (I Thess. 4:16-17). This will be the first event when Christ returns. The awakening shout will likely come from Christ himself, resulting in the resurrection of the dead in Christ and the transformation and gathering unto Him of the believers alive at that time. But the Archangel, too, will be heard. We do not know what he will say. But this being the time of victory, it may well be that the angel will break forth in a shout of victory for which the universe has been waiting.

2. The elect of Israel will be especially protected by the angels. This particular responsibility of the angels provides the student of the Bible with a very interesting subject. In the Old Testament we are told: "And at that time shall Michael stand up, the great prince which standeth for the children of thy people: and there shall be a time of trouble, such as never was since there was a nation even to that same time: and at that time thy people shall be delivered, every one that shall be written in the book"

(Dan. 12:1). This was told to Daniel concerning the coming Great Tribulation. Daniel was told that the elect of Israel would be safe and protected under the leadership of Michael the Archangel. And how is this protection to be carried out? In the Book of the Revelation John tells us: "And I saw another angel ascending from the east, having the seal of the living God: and he cried with a loud voice to the four angels, to whom it was given to hurt the earth and the sea, saying, Hurt not the earth, neither the sea, nor the trees, till we have sealed the servants of our God in their foreheads. And I heard the number of them which were sealed: and there were sealed an hundred and forty and four thousand of all the tribes of the children of Israel" (Rev. 7:2-4).

The worst time for Israel is yet to come, when Satan will turn on all his fury against them through the Antichrist. But God's holy angels will enter the battle under Michael, and they will apply the seal of God's ownership and protection upon the elect, and not even the fury of Satan will be able to touch them.

3. Angels will carry out various judgments of God in the Last Day. This is one of the major themes of the entire Book of the Revelation. I would like to suggest to the reader that he read chapters 8, 9, and 10 of that book and pay special attention to all the angels will be doing. Jesus himself summed it up when He said: ". . . the harvest is the end of the world; and the reapers are the angels. . . . The Son of man shall send forth his angels, and they shall gather out of his kingdom all things that offend, and them that do iniquity; and shall cast them into a furnace of fire: there shall be wailing and gnashing of teeth (Matt. 13:39-42).

4. Holy angels will engage in a great warfare with Satan and his angels. "And there was war in heaven: Michael and his angels fought against the dragon; and the dragon fought and his angels, and prevailed not; neither was their place found anymore in heaven. And the great dragon was cast out, that old serpent, called the Devil, and Satan, which deceiveth the whole world: he was cast out into the earth, and his angels were cast out with him" (Rev. 12:7-9). Satan is the ruler of the air. He is the "Master spirit of the air" (Eph. 2:2 Goodspeed Translation). He still has access to heaven where he accuses God's children (cf. Rev. 12:10). This great battle which will be fought somewhere in outer space, will end Satan's rule of the air, and he will then be deprived of access to heaven. We cannot say with certainty just when this battle will be fought. Many Bible students believe that it will take place at the time of the resurrection and the rapture when the saints shall meet Christ in the air. Satan has fought many battles and won some of them, especially against man who has tried to meet him without God. But this battle will be completely lost by Satan to Michael and his angels.

5. All the holy angels will accompany Christ when He returns in glory. "For the Son of man shall come in the glory of his Father with his angels" (Matt. 16:27). "When the Son of man shall come in his glory, and *all* the holy angels with him" (Matt. 25:31). "When the Lord shall be revealed from heaven with his mighty angels" (II Thess. 1:7).

It appears that the whole host of heaven will be with Christ when He will come to take over as king of the whole earth. This does not surprise us, for they have waited a long time to see the ultimate fulfillment of the promise of victory which was first made in the Garden of Eden, and was oft repeated by God's prophets through the ages. Their Creator is to reign. This is what the Angel Gabriel had been commissioned to tell Mary in Nazareth: "And he shall reign over the house of David for ever; and of his kingdom there shall be no end" (Luke 1:33).

6. An angel will arrest and imprison Satan for a thousand years. "And I saw an angel come down from heaven, having the key of the bottomless pit and a great chain in his hand. And he laid hold of the dragon, that old serpent which is the Devil, and Satan, and bound him a thousand years, and cast him into the bottomless pit, and shut him up, and set a seal upon him . . ." (Rev. 20:1-3). Satan will be bound and imprisoned for the duration of Christ's reign on earth as king of the earth. This binding will take place at the end of the Great Tribulation, immediately after Christ has returned in glory. That arrest will be carried out by an angel of God.

PRACTICAL APPLICATIONS TO THIS CHAPTER

1. The wonder of His amazing grace! Christ was made "a little lower than the angels" so that He could bear the penalty of sin for us. The Creator was made lower than His creation when He became man. "Where sin abounded, grace did much more abound."

2. Since angels desire to look into the mysteries of the wisdom and grace of God as manifested in our salvation, "how shall we escape, if we neglect so great salvation?"

3. The special message of the angels for this age is that the Lord Jesus will return just as He departed. We do take this message literally; but do we take it SERIOUSLY?

CHAPTER THREE

The Angels
and You

THE CHAPTER OUTLINED:

  I. Angels and Their Relationship to Our Saviour
     1. Angels are informed when a person receives Christ
       as Saviour
     2. Angels rejoice when a person turns from sin to God
     3. Angels behold our Christian warfare

  II. Angels and God's Providence in the Believer's Life
     1. Angels sometimes guide God's people
     2. Angels protect and deliver God's people from danger
     3. Angels encourage and strengthen God's people
     4. Angels are present when the believer dies

SUGGESTED BACKGROUND DEVOTIONAL READING

Monday—Rejoicing in Heaven (Luke 15:1-10)
Tuesday—The Angel Arranged This Meeting (Acts 8:26-35)
Wednesday—"Call For Simon," Directed the Angel (Acts 10:1-8)
Thursday—Peter Delivered by an Angel (Acts 12:1-11)
Friday—The Angel's Message of Encouragement (Acts 27:18-26)
Saturday—Children and "Their Angels" (Matt. 18:1-14)
Sunday—The Angel as a Waiter (I Kings 18:1-8)

Angels have a very definite relationship to God's people today. The Word of God declares that they are "all ministering spirits, sent forth to minister for them who shall be heirs of salvation" (Heb. 1:14). Quite plainly this means that the angels are occupied with God-appointed ministrations or services for the benefit of those who will make up the company of God's redeemed. To my understanding this may include the possibility of the angels being active in the life of a person even before he is actually saved. I believe this was the case in my own life.

According to the Scripture reference quoted above, and according to other statements in the Word of God, we find that angels are not dominating people, but are serving us under God's direction. They are unseen as far as we are concerned, but so is the Holy Spirit and even the Lord Jesus. What a beautiful thought—God's angels are looking after me! This is not just a beautiful thought, it is a tremendous fact.

In this chapter we are going to take a careful look at the kind of service angels have performed for God's children in the past, as revealed in the Bible. There is good reason to believe that such services are still being carried out by the angels for God's people today, with one significant difference. Until the revelation of God toward man was completed as we have it in the Bible today, the Lord often demonstrated the validity of a new message by a miracle or visible appearance. It is no surprise to me that God should speak directly to Moses, or appear in visible form to Abraham and talk with him. They did not have a single line of written revelation. Miracles and angelic appearances continued through the early days of Christianity to confirm the gospel message as being God's message, exactly as Jesus had promised (cf. Mark 16:17-20). The New Testament was not yet written, and the disciples could not say: Turn to Matthew, chapter 27; or to Romans, chapter 5. They preached and taught a new message which had been promised in the Old Testament. The signs and miracles that followed them were God's endorsement of the message. To this heavenly endorsing of the new message belongs also the appearances of angels who carried out many of the miraculous acts of God in behalf of His people. When once the written record of God's Word was completed, public miracles and visible manifestations of angels ceased, or at least greatly decreased. We now do not need a miracle to endorse the Gospel, for we have the written Word for our authority. If men will not believe the Bible, they will not believe because of a miracle.

The Biblical indication is that the angels still carry out regular and special assignments for God, and these assignments include the miraculous and providential care of God for His people. However, except for rare occasions, angels do not now appear to man in visible form or perform miracles that are apparent to the public. I have never seen an angel as far as I know (though my wife insists I have lived with one for 40 years). But I have been aware of the special and even miraculous protection of the supernatural on a number of occasions. And based upon what the Bible says, I have good reason to believe that the angels were there to carry out God's design. I continually thank the Lord for this provision of His grace.

A closer study of what God has said about angels and their ministry to the saved presents us with the following fascinating facts:

I. Angels and Their Relationship to Our Salvation

1. Angels are informed when a person receives Christ as Saviour. "Also I say unto you, Whosoever shall confess me before men, him shall the Son of man also confess before the angels of God" (Luke 12:8).

Angels are important members of God's family. They are very much interested in the salvation of men and women because they know of the great price that made the salvation possible. They were the first to tell the good news of the Saviour's birth, as well as the news of His glorious resurrection. When a person confesses Christ publicly as his Lord and Saviour, our Lord publicly announces the news in heaven. He calls out our names before the angels. This is like a public announcement of our heavenly citizenship. This is a great honor, a wonderful truth to know. I am going to show this to the next person who wants to be saved, but hedges on confessing Him publicly.

2. Angels rejoice when a person turns from sin to God. "Likewise, I say unto you, there is joy in the presence of the angels of God over one sinner that repenteth" (Luke 15:10).

Bible students differ on whether the joy mentioned here is that of the Lord or of the angels. E. V. Rieu calls it "The jubilation of the angels" in his translation of the Gospels. I believe that our Lord really was talking about the whole family of God in heaven, which certainly would include the angels.

Nowhere in God's Word are we told that angels weep. But they do rejoice. They are glad when just one sinner turns from self and sin toward God. Perhaps they are glad because they know what a person is saved *from.* Perhaps they are glad because they know what a person is saved *for.* Perhaps they rejoice because a new child is born into the family of God and that calls for a celebration. One thing is certain, angels are interested in our salvation. About this our Lord left no doubt. Peter told us by inspiration that "the angels desire to look into" the mysteries connected with our salvation (cf. I Peter 1:12). Do we want to make heaven glad? We can do so by bringing one soul into contact with Jesus Christ.

3. Angels behold our Christian warfare. ". . . for we are made a spectacle unto the world, and to angels, and to men" (I Cor. 4:9).

The Greek word translated "spectacle" is *theatron,* from which we get our word "theater." The word appears only three times in the Greek New Testament, and in the other two instances it is translated "theatre" (cf. Acts 19:29, 31).

A theater is a place where people perform, and where others go to see them perform—to be spectators. Speaking of the struggles of the apostles in particular, Paul says that they "are a spectacle unto the world [universe], and to angels, and to men." This is true, not only of the apostles, but of all believers. Angels are looking on as we walk with the Lord. The world is also watching us. But angels look on with sympathy, interested in our victories through Christ, while the world is more interested in our failures and downfalls. Look up, you who are burdened in your Christian life with trials and temptations. The angels are looking on with sympathy, and they are pulling and rooting for you.

Does our behavior as Christians ever shock the angels? I believe that this is quite possible. Paul, by inspiration, exhorted Christian women to be careful in their conduct and appearance, "Because of the angels" (I Cor. 11:10). The context of this verse reveals that the apostle has been talking about recognizing and showing proper respect for God's order in His family. This order includes Christ as the head of the Church, and man as the head of the family. Here Paul is asking the ladies in the church to be careful regarding this matter. Of course, times and customs have changed in the 19 centuries that have passed into the tomb of time since then, but God's Word and the angels have not changed. They are still looking on with interest and great sympathy as God's children are growing up spiritually. They long for our spiritual health and welfare. They won't expect anything unreasonable. But let us not shock them with arrogant disregard of the Word of God and of that spirit of modesty which is becoming to the children of God. The angels are looking on. They may not be shockproof!

II. Angels and God's Providence in the Believer's Life

By the Holy Spirit's own definition, angels are "ministering spirits, sent forth to minister for them who shall be heirs of salvation" (Heb. 1:14). Though the rendering of this verse in the King James Version is quite plain, it is interesting and helpful to consider some other translations. Charles B. Williams renders it: "Are not the angels all attending spirits sent forth to serve for the sake of those who are going to be unceasing possessors of salvation?" The Twentieth Century New Testament reads: "Are not all the angels spirits in the service of God, sent out to minister for the sake of those who are destined to obtain salvation?"

The angels are the instruments or agents of God who carry out God's providential workings in the lives of those who make up the company of God's redeemed. The angels "attend" us. How do they attend or serve us? Let us take a close look into the Word of God and consider the various ways in which angels are active in our lives, unknown and unseen by us. They act as agents of God's providence, in small events and in big ones, for the purpose of accomplishing God's design—"Working all things together for good to them that love God, to them who are the called according to his purpose" (Rom. 8:28).

1. **Angels sometimes guide God's people**. "And the angel of the Lord spake unto Philip, saying, Arise, and go toward the south unto the way that goeth down from Jerusalem unto Gaza, which is desert" (Acts 8:26).

Philip was enjoying a successful evangelistic campaign in Samaria when an angel directed him to go into the desert. As Philip obeyed and went to the right place, the Holy Spirit took over. Philip was then able to unfold the plan of salvation to the treasurer of the queen of Ethiopia, while riding in luxury inside the treasurer's chariot.

An angel of God directed Cornelius to send for Simon Peter who was staying in Joppa. It was Peter who was then to explain to Cornelius God's way of salvation (cf. Acts 10:1-6, 22, 30). Here again we find that the angel and the Holy Spirit worked together. While the angel worked on Cornelius, the Holy Spirit worked on Peter (cf. Acts 10:19-20; 11:11-12). I believe it is both interesting and significant that in both cases of angelic guidance mentioned in these chapters, the angel guided in getting the seeker and the preacher together. Then the preacher brought the message (not the angel), while the Holy Spirit did His office work. This work was actually making the message of salvation effective in the lives of those who heard it.

While looking back over 40 years of gospel ministry, I am impressed with the number of meetings with individuals (some of whom are now ministers or missionaries) which were marked by very peculiar and remarkable circumstances. "Chance" meetings led to the conversion of those individuals. Did the angels have something to do with the timing of those unlikely circumstances? I like to believe that they did. Doubtless many of God's children can tell of similar experiences in their own lives. What surprises we will have when in the next life we become acquainted with all that God did in His wonderful providence to bring the message of salvation to those who would receive it! At the present time we may not know whether the Holy Spirit was at work, or whether an angel of God worked out the circumstances. It may well be that both did their part, for as we see revealed in the Word of God, they do work together in guiding our steps toward God's salvation.

2. **Angels protect and deliver God's people from danger.** "But the angel of the Lord by night opened the prison doors, and brought them forth" (Acts 5:19).

"And, behold, the angel of the Lord came upon him, and a light shined in the prison: and he smote Peter on the side, and raised him up, saying, Arise up quickly. And the chains fell off from his hands" (Acts 12:7).

An angel delivered the three friends of Daniel from the fiery furnace (cf. Dan. 3:25, 28). An angel protected Daniel during his night in the den of lions (cf. Dan. 6:21-22). Angels rescued Lot from the destruction of Sodom (cf. Gen. 19:15-16).

Many are the accounts in the Bible of God's angels taking a hand in protecting or delivering God's children from danger. Just because we do not see them now, does not mean they no longer perform such services. On the contrary, we may be sure that they do still protect and deliver from hidden dangers, because they are still God's ministering spirits. This particular service of the angels takes on special significance when we consider the fact that Satan and his host of demons are forever trying to injure God's people, both physically and spiritually. Jesus declared that Satan "was a murderer from the beginning" (John 8:44). We know that he tried to destroy Job, David, Daniel, Mordecai, Simon Peter, and Paul. Unless restrained, he would hurt every person who bears a testimony for the Lord. Demons seem forever desirous of hurting people. But God's holy angels are our protectors, unseen to us, but very real, carrying out God's providence in our behalf.

Jesus said of little children: "Take heed that ye despise not one of these little ones; for I say unto you, That in heaven *their angels* do always behold the face of my Father which is in heaven" (Matt. 18:10).

Is there any basis for the belief that children have guardian angels? Now, what else could our Lord have meant when He talked about "their angels"? The context of the verse reveals the fact that Jesus was emphasizing the importance of children to God. Seven times He mentioned children in His talk (Matt. 18:3-14). In verse 10 He stresses their importance by telling His disciples that their angels, who watch over them, are nearest to God's throne in heaven.

It appears that the Jews in Jesus' day, and the disciples in particular, believed that each of them had a special angel. When Peter was delivered from prison in the middle of the night, and knocked at the gate of the house where the disciples were still praying for his deliverance, a maid went to see who it might be. When she recognized Peter, she became so excited she forgot to open the gate, but ran back in the house and told what she had seen. They would not believe her and said she had lost her mind. When she kept on insisting that Peter was really out there, they said: "It is his angel" (Acts 12:14-15). They believed that Peter had an angel all his own.

But if little children have angels who watch over them, why do some children get hurt or killed? This is a fair question to which we find no easy answer. We might find the answer if we ask another question: Why did the angel deliver Peter from prison and certain death, when James suffered death by the sword? Where was his angel? The whole matter revolves around the sovereignty and infinite wisdom of God. We simply dare not question the goodness and the wisdom of God in all His providential dealings. God in His wisdom still had work for Peter to accomplish, and so He sent His angel to deliver him. On the other hand, the cause of Christ in the salvation of souls may have been better served by the martyrdom of James than by his life.

It would be the height of folly for us to expect the God of the universe to adjust His providential doings to our ideas, or even to our understanding. If no children would ever be hurt, parents would become careless, and God does not endorse carelessness or recklessness. I firmly believe that God's angel is watching over me while I drive through heavy traffic to visit someone in the hospital. The Lord promised: "The angel of the Lord encampeth round about them that fear him, and delivereth them" (Ps.

34:7). But I keep my hand on the wheel and my eyes on the road, driving carefully, for I also believe that if I should drive recklessly, the angel might jump off and let me learn my lesson.

While on the subject of angelic protection, I want to testify that I have experienced that protection consciously on a number of occasions. The reader is asked to bear with just one example.

During the years of World War II we lived in Washington, D.C., where I served as pastor of the First Brethren Church of that city. On a Monday afternoon in the spring of 1941 we took a drive toward the city of Baltimore. Sunday had been a very busy day and a little relaxation was needed. My wife and five-year-old daughter went along for the ride. There were no freeways and interstate roads in those days, and we drove out Bladensburg Road and old U.S. Highway 1, which was then the main road between Washington and Baltimore. When we arrived in the suburbs of Baltimore, we agreed we had gone far enough and decided to turn around. So I turned into a side street to my right at an intersection with a traffic light, turned around in the next block and came back to the intersection. The traffic light turned green for us just before we got to it, and I proceeded to make the left turn to get back on the highway toward home. Just at that moment a peculiar sensation gripped me which urged me to stop. I did not hear a voice audibly, but there was an inner voice which I can best describe as a compelling urge which said: "Stop." I did stop right in front of the green light which said: "Go." And just then a large truck came through the red light from our left at a very high rate of speed. Had I not stopped at the green light, we would likely have been three dead people in our car. What made me stop when the light said go? I do not remember of ever doing that deliberately, except on that day. I believe it was an angel from the Lord looking after us. We just sat there a bit, shook a little, and thanked the Lord for stopping us.

Most believers can tell of mysterious deliverances in their lives, which can only be explained by the recognition of divine providence. But what startling revelations will be ours when in that world to come we shall know fully, even as we are fully known. Then the veil which now hides the unseen world of spirits from our eyes will be removed, and we shall see how often the angels were busy protecting us from dangers. Then we shall see how they somehow hindered us when we would have rushed into some rash or evil purpose—like the angel stopped Balaam long ago (cf. Num. 22:31-32).

3. Angels encourage and strengthen God's people. "For there stood by me this night the angel of God . . . saying, Fear not, Paul; thou must be brought before Caesar: and, lo, God hath given thee all them that sail with thee. Wherefore, sirs, be of good cheer: for I believe God, that it shall be even as it was told me" (Acts 27:23-25).

Paul and the other 275 people on board of a sailing vessel were lost at sea. Driven by a fierce storm for several weeks, they had abandoned all hope of survival. Then an angel assured Paul in the night that all would be saved from the storm by being cast upon an island, and that he must appear before Caesar. Paul believed the angel's message as coming from God, and took courage. Subsequent events confirmed every word of the angel as being true.

Elijah was weary, exhausted, and completely discouraged. He wished to die. As he fell asleep under a juniper tree, an angel woke him up and set some food in front of him. The prophet ate and drank, and went back to sleep. After a good rest the angel awakened him again and brought him some special food which enabled Elijah to keep going for 40 days (cf. I Kings 19:4-8).

Looking back, I can remember some days when discouragement seemed to overwhelm me. Then some Barnabas (Son of consolation) came along who seemed to know just what I needed, and I was strengthened. Did one of God's angels have anything to do with this? Surely, God knew my need, and whom to send, and the angels are His serving spirits, sent forth to attend God's people.

4. Angels are present when the believer dies. "And it came to pass, that the beggar died, and was carried by the angels into Abraham's bosom . . ." (Luke 16:22).

Much has been said and written by Bible teachers on this chapter, insisting that we must not exploit the details of the parables of Jesus, that we must not build doctrines upon those details. This is doubtless true and I fully agree. But we must also bear in mind that whatever Jesus said, including the details, must be in harmony with the facts. If Jesus spoke of torment on the other side, there *is* torment there. Likewise, when Jesus said that the angels carried the beggar to his rest when he died, I simply believe that this is how it is, and I want to tell it as it is. I know Jesus would not mislead us about life after death. Did He not insist while speaking about that subject on another occasion: "If it were not so, I would have told you"? Furthermore, the thought that angels are attending the believer at the time of death is in complete harmony with the Holy Spirit's description of their work as "ministering spirits, sent forth to minister for them who shall be heirs of salvation." If the Lord should tarry a while with His coming, and I shall pass through the experience of death, I know I won't be alone. The angels will be waiting, and they know the way into the Lord's presence.

CHAPTER FOUR

Satan, the
Most Beautiful Angel

THE CHAPTER OUTLINED:

I. What Satan Is Not
   1. Satan is not ugly or hideous in appearance
   2. Satan is not omnipresent
   3. Satan is limited in power, he is not omnipotent
   4. Satan is limited in knowledge; he is not omniscient
   5. Satan is not in hell

II. The Origin of Satan — Where Did He Come From?
   1. Satan is a created being
   2. Satan was created a perfect being
   3. "The anointed cherub that covereth"

III. The Fall of Satan
   1. Satan sinned
   2. The nature of Satan's sin was that of rebellion against God

IV. The Results of Satan's Fall
   1. Some of the angels joined the rebellion
   2. Satan was judged and condemned to . . . the lake of fire
   3. Satan became the enemy of God
   4. Satan became totally evil

SUGGESTED BACKGROUND DEVOTIONAL READING

Monday—Why God Wants Us To Know about Satan (II Cor. 2:11; John 8:44)

Tuesday—Satan and His Ministers (II Cor. 11:13-15)

Wednesday—"Perfect . . . Till Iniquity Was Found" (Ezek. 28:11-17)

Thursday—"I Will . . . I Will . . . I Will . . . " (Isa. 14:12-15)

Friday—The Devil's Lies (Gen. 3:1-6)

Saturday—Standing Up to Satan's Tricks (Eph. 6:10-18)

Sunday—Devil Worship Will Be Worldwide (Rev. 13:4-15)

The purpose of the written revelation of God to man is to reveal the history of God's dealings with man, with the redemption of man through Jesus Christ as the central story. Therefore, the Triune God and man are the main actors in the unfolding of God's revelation.

Then there is Satan, the enemy of God and man, who seems to have his hand in everything. He turns up more often in the history of God's dealings with man than anyone else aside from God himself. Presented under more than 20 different titles, Satan has dominated the history of man more than any created being. He is called the "Prince" or "Chief Ruler" by the Son of God himself, while the Apostle Paul calls him "the god of this age [world]." John the apostle asserted that "the whole world lieth in the evil one." Satan is responsible for every sin, every death, every pain, every heartbreak, every crime, every tear, every war that has ever come upon mankind. There are four chapters in the Bible that describe the earth and the existence of man minus the presence and influence of Satan. Significantly they are the first two and the last two chapters of this inspired volume.

There are several things that we should understand clearly as we enter into a study of this evil person. The first of these is the fact that the only place where we can find out anything reliable about him is in the Bible. All other sources of information are not to be trusted unless they are based upon God's revelation in His Word. Human authors who have told the truth about Satan have received it from God's Word. Ignoring the revelation that God has given of him, man has made Satan appear as a weird figure. He is pictured with cloven hoof and horns, or just a figure of speech like Uncle Sam, or an invention of the imagination like Santa Claus. The Bible on the other hand gives us an inspired biography of Satan, including his origin, character, career, power, ambition, work, methods, and his final doom.

Another fact to remember as we enter upon this study is that God wants us to know about Satan. As one of our modern writers, McCandlish Phillips, said succinctly: "The Bible pointedly exposes Satan and exposes his tactics, for man's sake. Paul wrote that man must keep Satan from gaining the advantage over us; for we are not ignorant of his devices (II Cor. 2:11). The reverse of that is: If we remain ignorant of Satan's devices, he will gain the advantage over us. In plain fact, he already has gained such advantage especially over the young people of this nation. We can know nothing about Satan apart from the Scriptures. It is the Bible that reveals him to the understanding of man, and we need desperately to know about him because what Satan does, and how he does it, are the concealed factors behind present eruptions of evil in the world."

Yes, God wants us to know all He has revealed about Satan and his tactics so that we may "be able to stand against the wiles of the devil" (Eph. 6:11).

I. What Satan Is Not

In order to know all that we can about our enemy we should know about his limitations. There are ideas abroad about Satan which are not true. The following are some of the more important facts:

1. Satan is not ugly or hideous in appearance. A popular but grossly mistaken idea is that Satan is a grotesque being, hideous and repulsive in appearance. Quite the contrary is true. The Bible says that he was created "perfect in beauty," and that his heart was "lifted up because of thy [his] beauty" (Ezek. 28:12-17). The New Testament tells us that he "transformeth himself into an angel of light" (II Cor. 11:14 Lit. trans.).

2. Satan is not omnipresent. Only God is omnipresent. Satan is a created being and cannot be everywhere or even in two places at the same time. When given permission by the Lord to try Job, "Satan went forth from the presence of the Lord" (Job 1:12). "So went Satan forth from the presence of the Lord, and smote Job . . ." (Job 2:7). Peter warns us that our "adversary, the devil . . . walketh about, seeking whom he may devour" (I Peter 5:8). Satan may have his helpers well spread out, he may move from place to place with the speed of light, but he can only be in one place at a time.

3. Satan is limited in power, he is not omnipotent. He has great power over the forces of nature and even of death, but he is limited in the use of the power that he does have to the sovereign will of God. Without God's permission he could not have harmed Job, or sifted Peter, hindered Paul— nor can he hurt you. This is good to know when he tries to threaten you.

4. Satan is limited in knowledge; he is not omniscient. Satan does not know everything. He does not know the future. He does not know how you will respond when he tempts you. He figured that Job would curse God if he could discourage him enough with pain and trouble. He was pretty sure, but he was dead wrong. Satan has great knowledge. His wisdom is far greater than man's wisdom. He knows how to manage and manipulate people. He has long experience in this. He also knows what he plans to do. He therefore may be able to predict certain events involving the actions of human beings, with a fair degree of accuracy. But he does not foreknow the future aside from his own plans, and sometimes his plans backfire.

5. Satan is not in hell. Many people have the idea that the devil is in hell, is in charge of tormenting lost souls there, and that somehow he carries on his devilish work on earth from that place. Satan is not now in hell and has never yet been there. He will be put there after the thousand-year kingdom of Christ when his sentence there will begin as we are told in the Word of God. "And the devil that deceived them was cast into the lake of fire and brimstone, where the beast and the false prophet are, and shall be tormented day and night forever and ever" (Rev. 20:10).

Though removed from his high position and office in heaven when he sinned, and though condemned to spend eternity in the lake of fire that is prepared for him and his angels, Satan is free now to roam the universe and seems to have access to heaven itself. Repeatedly he is said to appear in the presence of God to slander and accuse God and man (cf. Job. 1:6-11; 2:1-7). Satan is called the "prince of the power of the air" (Eph. 2:2). The time will come when Satan and his angels will be cast out of heaven and "neither was their place found any more in heaven" (Rev. 12:7-9, 13). At that time he will turn all his fury on Israel. Until then he is free to go where he wants to go. This freedom can be seen in his appearance to Christ in the wilderness where he took Him up into a high mountain and on top of the pinnacle of the Temple.

II. The Origin of Satan — Where Did He Come From?

The Bible never argues for the existence of God but assumes that His existence is understood by all intelligent creatures. Without any introduction, God is brought majestically before us in the first sentence of the Bible in all His wisdom and power. "In the beginning God created the heaven and the earth."

In like manner, the Bible does not argue the existence of the devil, but proceeds upon the assumption that there can be no question about his being. And without argument or introduction Satan is brought before us in the third chapter of the Bible in all the crookedness and malice of his seductive nature. In his first appearance we find him contradicting God "Ye shall not surely die" and slandering God by insinuating that God's motive was mean and selfish: "God doth know that in the day ye eat thereof, then your eyes shall be opened, and ye shall be as gods . . ." (Gen. 3:4-5). There he deceived Eve, and he has been deceiving mankind ever since.

Although the Word of God assumes the existence of Satan, it sheds some light on the question of how he got to be what he is and where he is. Jesus told His disciples on one occasion: "I beheld Satan as lightning fall from heaven" (Luke 10:18), and that is where he came from—out of God's heaven.

There are two passages of Scripture which shed a great deal of light on Satan's original state and subsequent fall. The first of these is Isaiah 14:12-17. These verses are prophetic in nature and point to the final Babylon or world empire with its wicked head, the Antichrist. In verse 12 the description turns to Satan who will indwell the Antichrist.

The second passage to be studied here is found in Ezekiel 28:11-17. These verses have for their background the condemnation of God upon the king of Tyrus, a historical king, who pretended to be divine. Verse 11 passes from the human king to his spiritual master, Satan, who inspired and perhaps even possessed him. That these verses do not refer to the human king of Tyrus can easily be seen by considering what is said of him.

"Thou wast created." The only man created was Adam. All others are born, including kings. "Thou wast perfect in thy ways." This cannot be said of any man except the Son of Man, even Jesus. "Thou hast been in Eden, the garden of God." This was not true of any earthly king, but is true of Satan. There is no question in my mind about this being a description of the origin of Satan.

What can we learn from these verses about the beginning of Satan?

1. Satan is a created being. "Thou wast created" (Ezek. 28:13, 15). The Word of God clearly sets forth that all beings are created by God through the Son. This includes things "that are in heaven, and that are in earth, visible and invisible, whether they be thrones, or dominions, or principalities, or powers . . ." (Col. 1:16). There leaves no room for doubt—Satan is a created being.

2. Satan was created a perfect being. "Thou wast perfect in thy ways from the day that thou wast created" (Ezek. 28:15).

Satan was perfect in his original state. The word translated "perfect" (*tom* in the Hebrew) is also used of God's perfect ways as in II Samuel 22:31 and Psalm 18:30. Perhaps the best word in our language to fit its meaning is the word "blameless." Satan was not only perfect in his ways, he was created "perfect in beauty" (Ezek. 28:12). Here the Hebrew word translated "perfect" is *kalil* which means entirely or completely. Consider this person who became Satan! He was perfect in his ways and altogether beautiful. There is more, for we read: "Thou sealest up the sum, full of wisdom" (28:12). Satan in his original state was the full measure or the last word in perfection and full of wisdom.

3. **"The anointed cherub that covereth"** (Ezek. 28:14). Cherub is the singular of cherubim. The phrase "that covereth" speaks of protecting or guarding. It seems that Satan was of the order of heavenly beings known as cherubims, who are the guardians of the throne of God. The designation "the *anointed* cherub" strongly suggests that he was especially selected and favored by God as the leader of the heavenly host. This idea fits the overall description of Satan in the entire Bible.

Now let us put it all together and see what God has revealed about this wonderful creature. We behold here a heavenly being of the order of cherubims who is perfect in uprightness, altogether beautiful by heaven's standard, the last word in perfection and full of wisdom, anointed by God as the highest ranking leader in heaven. Add to all this his name "Lucifer" which means "Day Star" or "Shining One" (Isa. 14:12). This is the one who became Satan—the "wicked one," "murderer," the "father of lies," who "deceiveth the whole world." How can this be?

III. The Fall of Satan

"Thou wast perfect in thy ways *till . . .*" (Ezek. 28:15). One of the most important little words in the Bible is the word "until" or "till" as the old versions have it. Here it introduces the terrible fall of Lucifer from the highest level of perfection to the lowest level of evil.

1. **Satan sinned.** "Till iniquity was found in thee" (Ezek. 28:15). "And thou hast sinned" (v. 16). Here we are faced with one of the greatest mysteries of the Bible. The mystery is not what the sin of that anointed cherub was, for its nature is well documented. It was the sin of rebellion against God, the outgrowth of pride and false ambition; but more of that later.

The mystery about that fall which man has not been able to solve is

us a disgrace to God and unfitting us for the service of God. But we need not fear, for "greater is he that is in you, than he that is in the world" (I John 4:4). Let us not be guilty of being "ignorant of his devices," but let us put on the "whole armour of God," so that we "may be able to stand against the wiles of the devil" (Eph. 6:11).

CHAPTER FIVE

The Devil
and His Fingerprints

THE CHAPTER OUTLINED:

I. Satan Is the Owner and Mastermind of This World
1. This was Satan's own claim before the Son of God
2. Christ called Satan "the prince of this world"
3. The inspired writers present Satan as the ruler of this world

II. How Satan Became the Ruler of This World
1. God . . . appointed man to be in charge of life . . .
2. God gave man a free will . . . for trust and obedience
3. Satan proposed a . . . clear break with God
4. Our first parents yielded to Satan's proposal

II. Satan's Fingerprints Are Found on the World
1. Satan is a murderer, literally a "man slayer"
2. Satan is a liar
3. Satan is the sworn enemy of the Jew
4. Satan delights in blaspheming God

SUGGESTED BACKGROUND DEVOTIONAL READING

Monday—The Devil Offered a Trade (Luke 4:1-13)

Tuesday—The Great Conflict of the Ages (Gen. 3:14-15)

Wednesday—The Prince of This World (John 14:27-31)

Thursday—Satan's Blindfold (II Cor. 4:1-7)

Friday—"I Pray Not for the World" (John 17:4-9)

Saturday—In the World, but Not of It (John 17:12-18)

Sunday—The Worst Blasphemer (Rev. 13:1-6)

The devil owns and runs this world in which we live. This is a shocking statement but a true one. Jesus Christ confirmed it, and the Bible certainly presents Satan as the ruler and mastermind of this world. What is more, Satan's fingerprints can readily be seen on this world, showing his hand in its direction and course.

Before we take another step we must have an understanding as to what "world" we are talking about. There are at least three words in the Greek New Testament which are translated "world" in our English Bible. The two principle ones are *kosmos* and *aion*. Kosmos appears 187 times in the New Testament and in all but one instance is translated "world." The one exception is in I Peter 3:3 where it is translated "adorning." The word has various shades of meaning determined by its context, but basically it speaks of the order or arrangements in the world of people. It speaks not so much of the earth as the home of man, but of the order and organization that man has evolved, all the way up to our present complex human society. It almost always carries within its context the idea of this world system as being opposed to God, both in its nature and in its ways. Thus the Holy Spirit testifies: ". . . the whole world [kosmos] lieth in wickedness"; "Lieth in the wicked one" would be a more accurate translation (I John 5:19).

There are a few instances where kosmos is used of the people of the world without the world system, as in John 3:16 where we are told that "God so loved the world [kosmos]." God does love all the people that make up the world, but He does not love the world system in which they live. It was this world system which crucified the Son of God.

This kosmos world is the vast system of man's civilization which has worlds within worlds. Included in this system is a political world, a social world, an industrial world, a religious world, and a commercial world. It includes a world of music, a world of sports, a world of art, a world of literature. This world has a place for everything and for everyone—almost! There is a place in it for the moral man, the cursing man, the praying man, the lustful man, the benevolent man, the industrial man, the drinking man, the sober man, the rich man, and the poor man. Yes, there is a place in this world for everyone except the Son of Man. For Him there was no place in the inn when He was born into this world. The world had no place for Him in its politics, in its society or in its religion. "He was in the world, and the world knew him not" (John 1:10). Even so today the world has no place for Him in its politics, business, culture, education, in its World Courts or its United Nations.

The Greek word *aion* which also is translated "world" in the New Testament actually speaks of a certain age. When used of "this present world" or "age," it seems to be speaking particularly of the kosmos or world system of this present dispensation in which we are living, and which will end with the return of Jesus Christ. The believer is warned not to love this world system because he has been delivered from it (Gal. 1:4). He does not belong to it, even though living in it as an ambassador of Christ (cf. John 17:14-16; James 4:4; I John 2:15-17).

I. Satan Is the Owner and Mastermind of This World

1. This was Satan's own claim before the Son of God. "And the devil, taking him up into an high mountain, shewed unto him all the kingdoms of the world in a moment of time. And the devil said unto him, All this power will I give thee, and the glory of them: for this is delivered unto me; and to whomsoever I will give it. If thou therefore wilt worship me, all shall be thine" (Luke 4:5-7). It is beyond the scope of this chapter to fully discuss the Temptation of Christ. Here I simply call attention to the fact of Satan's claim that the kingdoms of this world belong to him, that they were delivered to him, and that he has the right to do with them as he pleases. Apparently he was telling the truth because Jesus doubtless would have disputed the claim if it had been false.

2. Christ called Satan "the prince of this world." "Now is the judgment of this world: now shall *the prince of this world* be cast out" (John 12:31). "Of judgment, because *the prince of this world* is judged" (John 16:11; cf. John 14:30).

Three different times in the last day or two before His crucifixion our Lord named Satan the prince of this kosmos, the world system. The word "prince" means the chief leader or manager.

3. The inspired writers present Satan as the ruler of this world. "But if our gospel be hid, it is hid to them that are lost: In whom *the god of this world* hath blinded the minds of them that believe not, lest the light of the glorious gospel of Christ, who is the image of God, should shine unto them" (II Cor. 4:3-4). Here the Greek word *aion* is used by the apostle, and it should properly be translated: "The god of this age," because Paul refers to the world system of this present age of which Satan is declared to be the "god." There are a number of Scripture passages which at least imply that this world system belongs to Satan, and that he directs its course. The reader should carefully read Ephesians 2:2; and I John 5:19.

At this juncture it should be understood that Satan's control of the world and its governments is not absolute, for God is in control of the devil. Therefore, Satan's control is subject to the boundaries of God's sovereign will. This limitation is seen in his control of human government where God rules and overrules. "For there is no power but of God: the powers that be are ordained of God" (Rom. 13:1). We also must remember that man has a free will and is free to obey the will of God instead of the will of Satan.

II. How Satan Became the Ruler of This World

This is one of the saddest stories of the Bible which is recorded on its first pages. The blunt truth of it is that man sold out to the devil who then cheated man out of his dominion by a crooked deal. This is what Satan was talking about when he told Christ that the kingdoms of this world were his because they were "delivered unto him."

This doubtless was the worst deal man ever made, and is duplicated only by the bargain Judas made when he agreed to betray the Lord for 30 pieces of silver; a transaction which also was inspired by Satan (cf. John 13:1-2). While endeavoring to understand the whole situation of the scheme whereby Satan gained control of the world, we should consider the following facts as they are revealed in the Word of God:

1. **God created man and appointed him to be in charge of life on this planet** (Gen. 1:26-28). God told man to "have dominion" over His creation on this earth. God turned the earth over to man who was to act as God's administrator, subject to God's will. In the New Testament the inspired writer tells us: "Thou madest him [man] a little lower than the angels . . . and didst set him over the works of thy hands: Thou hast put *all things in subjection* under his feet" (Heb. 2:7-8). God placed man in charge of life on earth.

2. **God gave man a free will and called on him for trust and obedience.** God put man to the test of obedience by forbidding him to eat of the tree of the knowledge of good and evil and warned that disobedience would bring death (Gen. 2:16-17). Man's career was to be that of ruler of this world while walking in harmony with God.

3. **Satan proposed a different course to man, calling for a clear break**

with God. To persuade man to rebel against God, Satan followed a masterful plan which called for the planting of suspicion, the hiding of an outright lie under an umbrella of truth, and the glowing promise of tremendous gain. The story of all this is told in a few short sentences in Genesis, chapter 3, verses 1-7.

The planting of suspicion was in Satan's suggestion that God had a selfish motive in keeping Adam and Eve from the forbidden tree. The lie was that they would not die if they ate the fruit, thus also implying that God had lied to them. The glowing promise was that they would be like *Elohim.* To "be as gods [God]"—that was Satan's bait. He promised man more than God had promised. Satan always uses an alluring bait, except when he tempts man to take God's name in vain. He gets man to do that for nothing.

4. Our first parents yielded to Satan's proposal. They took the fatal plunge, used their God-given power of choice and rebelled against God. By obeying Satan, they accepted his leadership. This choice resulted in awesome consequences to which not only they, but all their natural descendants became subject. One of those consequences was that man and man's world came under the control of Satan who has tried ever since to get mankind to carry out his evil program of total opposition to God.

In the light of all this, Satan's temptation of Christ takes on new significance. Satan gained control of man's dominion on earth when man yielded to him. But Christ had dominion of the whole universe, including heaven. If Satan could get Christ to worship him, would he not have gained control of Christ's domain? It seems that Satan wanted to trade Christ the kingdoms of this world for Christ's dominion. We may well shudder at such daring, but Satan's philosophy has ever been that: "Every man has his price." Adam and Eve, Esau, Samson, David, and Judas Iscariot seemed to prove him right. In Christ Satan more than met his match. Christ did not take the bait, did not take the plunge, and went on to redeem the earth by giving himself as a sacrifice for the rebellion of man. And one day (pray that it may be soon) "the kingdoms of this world will become the kingdoms of our Lord, and of his Christ; and he shall reign for ever and ever" (Rev. 11:15). The right to rule the earth is Christ's because He redeemed the domain which man had forfeited to Satan. When Christ returns, Satan will be bound and Christ will rule the earth in righteousness and peace for a thousand years.

III. Satan's Fingerprints Are Found on the World

One day while I was meditating on the revelation that Satan directs the course of this world, the thought came to me that if this is true then the world ought to display the same characteristics that mark its master. The thought provoked me into drawing up two lists, one containing the outstanding characteristics of the world, and the other showing the characteristics of Satan and of the Antichrist whom he will possess and use. The result was quite startling. To me it was unmistakable proof of the inspiration of the Word of God. Each of these characteristics is a peculiar phenomenon for which there is no reasonable explanation aside from the Word of God. Each of these characteristics is also found in the personality and nature of Satan. These characteristics are: War and destruction of human lives; deception on every level; Anti-Semitism; blasphemy, taking God's name in vain. Let us look at these characteristics one by one, and from a different position by looking at the characteristics of Satan.

1. Satan is a murderer, literally a "man slayer" (cf. John 8:44). Jesus declared that the devil is a murderer from the beginning. He loves to kill. He delights in having human life destroyed. God is the author of life. Satan seeks to destroy life. This has been true of him from the beginning of human life on earth.

No sooner had the first natural children grown to manhood when Satan corrupted the one and led him to kill his brother Abel. Now, the Bible says that this murderer, who delights in seeing human life destroyed, is the god of this world, its prince and ruler. He directs the course of this kosmos. If this is true, then we may logically expect that this world, too, displays a characteristic destruction of human life. Is this the case? Nothing can be more obvious. Wars, violence and destruction have marked the path of human history. The more enlightened man has become, the more destructive have been the wars.

In World War II all the science and all the resources of the whole world were employed to kill people. This was done by bullet, bomb, bayonet, torpedo, fire, grenade, tank, mines, boobytraps, by jet and missile, by Atom bomb, until this earth was soaked with the blood of a hundred million human beings who died in the wake of war. I was very fortunate in that I had left my native Germany just before Hitler took over as dictator. The rest of my family remained there and suffered through that war. As a result, my youngest brother was killed as a member of the German army in

Russia. My youngest sister's husband was killed in Russia. My brother's eldest son was killed in Russia. Six of my first cousins were killed, all in the Russian "Meatgrinder."

We might expect that man would gradually learn to avoid war. (There has not been a lack of effort to prevent war.) After all, there is nothing more stupid than war. There have been peace conferences and anti-war machines. We have had a League of Nations which was to prevent war, and in more recent times we have a great United Nations. And yet, there is no end of stupid, killing wars. Why this stupid slaughter? It is because Satan pulls the strings and maneuvers situations so as to pit nation against nation. War is his fingerprint on this world. There is not going to be an end to wars until Satan is bound and put away. "And he laid hold on the dragon, that old serpent which is the Devil, and Satan, and bound him for a thousand years, and cast him into the bottomless pit, and shut him up, . . . that *he should deceive the nations no more*, till the thousand years be fulfilled" (Rev. 20:2-3). "And when the thousand years are expired, Satan shall be loosed out of his prison, and *shall go out to deceive the nations . . . ,* Gog and Magog, *to gather them together to battle"* (Rev. 20:7-8).

During the thousand years of Satan's confinement, there will be peace on earth when the world's armaments will be converted into agricultural machinery and all the world's armies will be sent home (cf. Isa. 2:4). As soon as Satan will be turned loose, once more he will immediately deceive the nations and lead them into battle. His character will still be that of a murderer. Destruction of life is his fingerprint and it shows.

2. Satan is a liar. He "abode not in the truth, because there is no truth in him. When he speaketh a lie, he speaketh of his own: for *he is a liar*, and the father of it" (John 8:44).

Satan lies. His strong characteristic is that of deceit. The Word of God uses such descriptions of his character as: "Satan, which deceiveth the whole world" (Rev. 12:9); he "deceives the nations" (Rev. 20:3, 8); he "blinds" people's minds to deceive them about God's wonderful salvation (II Cor. 4:4). The Bible speaks about Satan's wiles (cf. Eph. 6:11). A wile is a trap set with deception. We are warned about Satan's devices (cf. II Cor. 2:11).

With deceit Satan led the first couple into rebellion against God. Follow his trail through the pages of the Bible and you will find that wherever he has conquered, he has done so by deceit. He advertises supposed advantages in glowing terms while cunningly hiding the sad consequences. Whereas Christ is "the truth," Satan is a liar. When he entered into Judas, we find that man betraying Jesus with a kiss. Satan put into the hearts of Ananias and Sapphira the idea of lying to the Holy Spirit (cf. Acts 5:3).

As we look at the world system today we cannot help but see that deceit is its trademark. The whole political structure is shot through with deceit—on local, state, national, and international levels. The so-called social structure of this world is covered with thick layers of deceptions and pretense. There is make-believe everywhere. The commercial side of the world is overflowing with fraudulence of many kinds, especially in its advertising of goods and services. It hides the defects, while describing supposed advantages in glowing terms. It is designed to fool the public. Consider the advertising of intoxicating liquor as an example: Its effects are both degrading and destructive. It has killed thousands because of drinking drivers. It has wrecked millions of homes. And how is it advertised? Under the sign of the skull and crossbones, as it ought to be? Not so! You will find it advertised under the sign of beautiful roses and pretty feathers, with the good news that its sweet blends and aristocratic tastes will make its users men of distinction.

We clearly see Satan's mark of deceit in the religious realm of the world. With disgust and dismay we note his accomplishment of supplanting Christ with a make-believe Santa, and Christmas with Xmas (I hate to write the word). The Risen Lord of Easter has been dislodged by an Easter bunny. All this serves to effectively hide the reality of the Son of God coming into this world. We recognize Satan's fingerprint of deceit. He is a liar, and he masterminds the course of this world.

3. **Satan is the sworn enemy of the Jew.** This hatred is predicted in the first great prophetic Scripture. "And I will put enmity between thee and the woman, and between thy seed and her seed; it [*he* in the Hebrew] shall bruise thy head, and thou shalt bruise his heel" (Gen. 3:15). The great conflict of the ages between Satan and his children and the woman and her children is found here in embryo. The "seed of the woman" points straight to Christ who ultimately is to crush Satan's head. The Christ was to come into the world through Israel, and of woman without a human father. The moment God called Abraham aside to become the father of the people through whom He would bring the Redeemer, Satan's hatred was focused upon that people, and he plotted their destruction.

In the 12th chapter of the Revelation the terrible "enmity" is presented in a dramatic picture that enfolds both the past and future raging of Satan against Israel. This picture is called the "great wonder." The reader is asked to read this chapter carefully, especially verses 1-6, and verse 13.

The "woman" in this chapter is Israel who brought forth the "man child," who obviously is Christ. This Christ is caught up "unto God, and to his throne." But this Christ is to return and rule all nations. In the meantime Satan turns on his full fury upon the woman, Israel. This fury will be greatest in the time just preceding the return of Christ.

Satan hates the Jew. This is one of his agelong characteristics. Does the world which he rules and directs have such a characteristic? You do not need me to tell you that such is the case. Anti-Semitism is an agelong phenomenon for which there is no reasonable explanation until we look into the Word of God. We are taught in the Bible that Anti-Semitism is Satan-inspired. Once there was a Pharaoh who ordered that every male child born in Israel should be killed. God intervened and delivered Israel from extinction. Later on a man named Haman tricked the emperor of Persia, then ruler over all the civilized world, into signing a decree which called for the execution of every Jew in the world. God stepped in and Israel was saved. A Herod once ordered the killing of all boys of two years and younger in the environs of Bethlehem. Seventy years later Titus moved a Roman army into Palestine and after a long and bitter contest one and a quarter million Jews perished.

What has happened to the Jews during the last 1,900 years is a history within history. Again and again Anti-Semitism has raised its ugly head and caused the slaughter of people guilty of being born Jews. The histories of Poland, Spain, England, Germany, and Russia are filled with repeated bloodbath and severe persecutions of its Jews. Sometimes persecutions were carried on in the name of Christ, which must have pleased the devil exceedingly. Hitler's brief appearance upon the world scene brought death to millions of Jews. Nor was that terrible outburst of Satanic rage the end of Anti-Semitism. The smoldering volcano erupts every now and then, and politicians scramble to put the lid back on if they can. According to the Bible, the worst is yet to come when Satan will enter into the "man of sin," the Antichrist. He will try to exterminate Israel in what our Lord called the "great tribulation, such as was not since the beginning of the world to this time, no, nor ever shall be" (Matt. 24:21).

Why this hatred? There is nothing like it in all the world. There is abuse of the weak by the strong, but worldwide and agelong hatred and murder is something else. This is a spiritual phenomenon, having its origin with the devil. Anti-Semitism is his fingerprint upon the world.

Something that is usually overlooked is the fact that whenever the Jews are hated and persecuted, there true Christianity receives the same treatment, yes, even when it comes in the name of Christ. It is sad but true that even some beguiled believers in Christ are misled into despising the Jew. Let us remember that whoever joins in any way the world's antagonism toward Israel is playing right into the hands of Satan and is doing his bidding. Christian, beware!

4. Satan delights in blaspheming God. "O God, how long shall the adversary reproach? shall the enemy *blaspheme thy name for ever*?" (Ps. 74:10). "And the beast which I saw was like unto a leopard, and his feet were as the feet of a bear, and his mouth as the mouth of a lion: and the dragon gave him his power, and his seat, and great authority. . . . And there was given unto him *a mouth speaking great things and blasphemies. . . . And he opened his mouth in blasphemy against God, to blaspheme his name, and his tabernacle, and them that dwell in heaven*" (Rev. 13:2, 5-6).

Satan hates God and delights in having humans call God names. When Satan's man, the Antichrist, will come into power, sponsored and enabled by Satan, he will do all that Satan wants him to do. He will seek to destroy Israel and will marvelously blaspheme God, God's name, God's tabernacle, and those that are in heaven. So vile, so prolific will be his verbal abuse of all that points to God that even the unregenerate world will be astonished. That will have to be something awful, for it seems that nothing could shock this world when it comes to blasphemy.

Does the world show forth this characteristic of Satan? Does it bear his fingerprint? Is the world given to taking God's name in vain? With our heads hanging in shame we have to admit that the language of the world today is permeated with blasphemy, with the abuse of God's name, the name of Jesus Christ, the attributes of God, and of everything that is holy. Blasphemy is now freely used in the printed page and on the programs of news and entertainment. Taking God's name in vain is a national pastime and is part of the language of presidents, generals, teachers, housewives, and school children.

Why do people take God's name in vain? There is no biological, historical, scientific or psychological reason or explanation for this strange phenomenon. There is a spiritual explanation that fully accounts for it, and that is the fact that Satan desires man to abuse God's name, and being the mastermind of the world system, he gets this done with a vengeance. Every human being who uses God's name, or the name of Christ carelessly or thoughtlessly, is doing what the devil wants him to do, and the devil gets man to do it for nothing.

It is good to know some of the fingerprints of Satan on the world system which he directs and inspires. The Word of God is very emphatic in telling us that the person who has received Christ as Saviour and Lord, is saved out of this world, does not belong to its system, and therefore should not be conformed to it (cf. Gal. 1:4; John 17:14-16; Rom. 12:1-2). The Redeemed of God constitute an embassy in the midst of an evil world, bearing witness to Jesus Christ who gave His life to make possible our translation from the kingdom of darkness into the kingdom of righteousness.

CHAPTER SIX

The Devil Unmasked by the Son of God

THE CHAPTER OUTLINED:

I. The Exposure of Satan by His Titles
1. "Satan"
2. "The Devil"
3. "Beelzebub"
4. "The Enemy"
5. "The Wicked One"
6. "The Prince of This World"
7. "A Murderer from the Beginning"
8. "A Liar and the Father of It"

II. Jesus Exposed the Methods by Which Satan Operates
1. Satan steals away the Word of God
2. Satan plants imposters
3. Satan has a kingdom of evil spirits
4. Satan's fatherhood
5. Satan, the sifter of men

SUGGESTED BACKGROUND DEVOTIONAL READING

Monday—Stealing the Word (Matt. 13:3-4, 18-19)

Tuesday—Impostors and Their Purpose (Matt. 13:24-30, 36-39)

Wednesday—Manifested to Destroy the Devil's Works (I John 3:1-8)

Thursday—The Devil As the Accuser (Job 1:11; Rev. 12:10)

Friday—"Harden Not Your Hearts" (Heb. 3:7-13)

Saturday—The Sifting of Simon Peter (Luke 22:31-34)

Sunday—"And Peter" (Mark 16:1-7)

One of the most stimulating and enlightening studies that any of us can engage in is to consider the entire encounter between the Son of God and Satan. This encounter led to the complete defeat of the devil. The Word of God explicitly declares that the Son of God became man in order to counteract the work of Satan and to utterly defeat him. The Holy Spirit declares through John: "He that committeth sin is of the devil; for the devil sinneth from the beginning. For this purpose the Son of God was manifested, that he might destroy the works of the devil" (I John 3:8). The writer of Hebrews said: "Forasmuch then as the children are partakers of flesh and blood, he [Christ] also himself likewise took part of the same; that through death he might destroy him that hath the power of death, that is, the devil; And deliver them who through fear of death were all their lifetime subject to bondage" (Heb. 2:14-15). In both the above passages the word translated "destroy" means to make powerless.

One way by which our Lord took away the power of the devil is by completely exposing him. Most of what we know of the devil has been revealed by Christ during His earthly ministry. Although we must keep in mind that Jesus did not supply information about the unseen world of spirits simply to satisfy human curiosity. He, nevertheless, exposed the devil as to what he is and how he operates. This chapter is devoted to the consideration of that exposure.

I. The Exposure of Satan by His Titles

Our Lord used a number of descriptive names or titles which graphically set forth the true nature of the devil. The list includes the following:

1. "Satan" (Matt. 4:10; 12:26; and others). Jesus used this name more often of the devil than any other, on at least nine different occasions. It is really a Hebrew word which had become part of the Greek language by that time. The word was well known to the Jews in those days. The name literally means "adversary." The devil is the hateful adversary or antagonist of both God and man. No mercy can ever be expected from him.

2. "The Devil"—*Diabolos* in Greek (cf. Matt. 13:39; Luke 8:12). This title means "the false accuser," or "slanderer," and was used by Christ on at least five different occasions. Satan accuses falsely, slanders, slurs, and denounces both God and man.

It is interesting to note that almost every time Satan speaks in the Scriptures, he is either accusing God or man, or both. In Eden he talked to

Eve and insinuated that God was not good. He accused God of acting selfishly in forbidding our first parents to eat of the tree of the knowledge of good and evil. Then he completed his accusation by implying strongly that God had deliberately lied when He warned them they would die if they ate of the forbidden tree. What a colossal slander of God! Yet, Satan managed to make it all look very reasonable to Eve.

The next time we hear Satan speak in the Bible, he is talking to God. Now we hear him accusing man to God. The old patriarch, Job, was a godly man who loved righteousness, trusted God, and hated sin (cf. Job 1:1). When the Lord asked Satan whether he had considered this, Satan began to slander Job by insinuating (he always seems to be insinuating something) that the patriarch served God purely from a selfish motive. "Doth Job fear God for nought? Hast not thou made an hedge about him, and about his house, and about all that he hath on every side? Thou hast blessed the work of his hands, and his substance is increased in the land. But put forth thine hand now, and touch all that he hath, and he will curse thee to thy face" (Job 1:9-11).

In the language of our day, Satan told the Lord that the reason Job was true to God was because he was eating steak. Satan saw the blessing of God upon Job. He saw God's hedge of providence around him. He thought he knew that Job did not serve the Lord out of sincerity, but because it paid to be good. Furthermore, Satan was sure he could prove this if he would be given that opportunity. When the Lord gave His permission to try Job's sincerity by destroying all of the patriarch's earthly possessions, Satan found out that he had been wrong. Then he came back with another accusation, or rather, insinuation: "Skin for skin, yea, all that a man hath will he give for his life" (Job 2:4). He still insisted that Job's faith was not real, and that he would prove it if he were permitted to touch the man's body. Thus we see that he really is the "Diabolos," the devil, the maligner, the slanderer, the false accuser. In the Book of the Revelation we read that there was loud rejoicing in heaven when John was shown a preview of Satan's final expulsion from heaven: "For *the accuser* of our brethren is cast down, which accused them before our God day and night" (Rev. 12:10).

3. **"Beelzebub"** (Matt. 12:24-27). This is a terrible name which literally would mean "the dung-god." It was used to emphasize the fact that Satan is the master who presides over all moral and spiritual corruption. Think of all the corruption that permeates human society today in its conversations,

its books, and its eruption of pornographic pictures. The devil is the master who presides over it all.

4. "The Enemy" (Matt. 13:39). Though an entirely different word, its meaning is about the same as the title "Satan," meaning an adversary, one who is against us. It emphasizes the idea of hatred and intent to do harm.

5. "The Wicked One" (Matt. 13:19, 38). The devil is wickedness or evil personified. This is the way in which our Lord used the title, "the wicked one." Satan is totally evil. Whereas "God is light, and in him is no darkness at all" (I John 1:5), Satan is darkness, and in him is no light at all.

6. "The Prince of This World" (John 12:31, 14:30). A very significant title, exposing the fact that Satan is the one who guides the unregenerate world system in its course which is away from the true God.

7. "A Murderer from the Beginning" (John 8:44). The title unmasks Satan as a fiend, a destroyer of human life. The Greek literally says "man slayer." For further study I refer the reader to the previous chapter where this title is dealt with at some length.

8. "A Liar and the Father of It" (John 8:44). Here is a summary of Satan's evil and crooked nature. "There is no truth in him," said Jesus. He even lies when he tells the truth because he will be using the truth to deceive by mixing a little poison of deceit with it, using the truth as a decoy. This designation by Jesus stamps Satan as being totally evil and malicious, incapable of using the truth except it be for an evil purpose. Whereas God "cannot lie" (Titus 1:2), "there is no truth in him [Satan]."

II. Jesus Exposed the Methods by Which Satan Operates

This particular study should prove of special interest to all who are in any way concerned about the salvation of the lost. From what Jesus said about Satan's activities, we get the very strong impression that the devil concentrates his main efforts and cunning upon an all-out endeavor to keep people from turning to God through faith in Jesus Christ. He will do anything to keep people from being saved.

1. Satan steals away the Word of God. "When any one heareth the word of the kingdom, and understandeth it not, then cometh the wicked one, and catcheth away that which was sown in his heart" (Matt. 13:19).

The "understandeth it not" points to the person's heart which has become hard or insensible to spiritual truth by the constant influences of the world. Such a person does not easily recognize his need of salvation and so the Word does not readily penetrate the surface. To make sure that it does not enter the consciousness, Satan quickly snatches the Word away so that the person could not tell you afterwards what has been said.

It is a good thing that our Lord fully interpreted this parable for us or we would surely have missed the point. As Richard C. Trench, one of the ablest commentators on the Lord's parables has pointed out: "How natural it would have been to interpret 'the fowls' impersonally, as signifying in a general way, worldly influences hostile to the truth. How almost inevitably, if left to ourselves, we would have so done. Not so however our Lord. He beholds the kingdom of evil as it counterworks the kingdom of God, gathered up in a personal head, the 'Wicked One'."

Thus we learn that the devil comes to church wherever possible to steal away the gospel message from the hearers. Of course, we understand that he cannot be in every place, but he has his "fowls"—a whole kingdom of evil spirits to implement his purpose. His methods of preventing the Word to enter people's hearts vary with the situation.

Satan keeps the Word from having an entrance in the hearts of the unsaved by causing people around them to carry on a little whispering. This is done to distract attention. Not that the whisperers are aware of that, but the devil loves to use saints to do his work. He will do anything to distract the attention of the unsaved. I have often wondered whether he pinches the babies to cry at just the most important moment. Why is it that most disturbances happen just before or during the invitation? Satan also tries to occupy the minds of the unsaved during a gospel hour by having them think about their problems, their work, their business, or anything else that will keep the mind occupied. He will gladly use a church member who keeps looking at his watch, thus showing the unsaved how bored he is. But the main point of the story is that behind all of this is the devil who does not want any hearer to find his way to the Saviour.

In Luke's recording of this parable and the Lord's interpretation the additional clause, "lest they should believe and be saved," is found (8:12). This plainly tells us Satan's main objective. He wants to keep people from being saved. To this end he uses the whole kingdom of evil spirits who are subject to him. He also uses people, yes, he even uses saved people when possible. He uses circumstances, events, the forces of nature, emotions and reactions of those who hear the truth, to turn them off, "lest they should believe and be saved." Pastors, evangelists, teachers, soul winners, take note of how great is our need for earnestness, for prayer, for complete dependence on the Holy Spirit in our sacred task!

2. Satan plants imposters. "The field is the world [kosmos]; the good seed are the children of the kingdom; but the tares are the children of the wicked one; the enemy that sowed them *is the devil;* the harvest is the end of the world [aion or age]; and the reapers are the angels" (Matt. 13:38-39).

The writer is well aware of the theological battles that have raged around the interpretation of this parable. Those we need not enter into here. I must call the reader's attention to the fact that in verse 38 Jesus speaks of the field as being the kosmos, the whole world of people, while in verse 39 He uses the word aion, or age, saying that "the harvest is the end of the age." It is unfortunate that the King James Version does not make this distinction. This parable must refer to the kingdom of God during this age which will end at the Rapture when the Lord will come for His own.

In this interpretation of His parable of the wheat and the tares our Lord masterfully exposes the subtle and cunning ways of Satan. We learn from the interpretation that Satan, with malice in his heart, is the enemy of the Son of Man. He is presented as sneaking secretly "while men slept" into the field where the Lord has His children of righteousness, and right among those children of God, the devil hides his own children.

The main point of the whole parable seems to be the revelation that Satan works by imitating, by counterfeit, by using impostors. He sows tares among the wheat. The tares look exactly like wheat as long as wheat is in the blade. Therefore man cannot get rid of it for fear of destroying the wheat. The purpose of the tares is to hinder the growth of the wheat and greatly reduce the yield or harvest.

Does Satan secretly plant his children right among God's children? Do these emissaries of the devil look much like God's children so that you cannot tell them apart? The answer to both questions is positive. Both are true to a remarkable degree.

Consider Christ's own apostles to whom He explained the parable: One of them was an impostor, a counterfeit, an agent of Satan, all along. The other eleven apostles did not know it. They did not even suspicion it. This is demonstrated by the fact that when Jesus finally told them one would betray Him, they all kept asking: "Lord, is it I?" (cf. Matt. 26:21-22). Although the apostles did not know who the traitor was, Jesus knew it from the very beginning. Early in His ministry He warned: "Have not I chosen you twelve, and one of you is a devil?" (John 6:70). Yes, Satan had his secret agent planted right within the inner circle of Christ's followers. Judas must have looked and acted like the real thing. He was a successful counterfeit.

Imitation is Satan's favored method, and he still uses it with success today. He has his secret agents placed in the most strategic places such as seminaries, pulpits, and on church boards. The Word of God warns us: "For such are false apostles, deceitful workers, transforming themselves into the apostles of Christ. And no marvel; for Satan himself is transformed into an angel of light. Therefore it is no great thing if his ministers also be transformed as the ministers of righteousness . . ." (II Cor. 11:13-15).

Satan has his own "ministers." The worst enemy of the Gospel is not the outspoken atheist or infidel, but the agent of Satan who uses pious phrases until he becomes a person of influence. By the time his true nature is apparent, he has poisoned many minds and caused confusion and consternation within the family of God's children.

The greatest counterfeit of Satan will be the awful trinity of evil that he will set up in the days of the Great Tribulation. Satan himself as god, the Antichrist as Christ, and the False Prophet of Revelation 13 as representing the Holy Spirit. The reader is urged to read such Scripture passages as II Thessalonians 2:1-12; and Revelation, chapter 13. The passage in II Thessalonians tells us that Antichrist will come "after the working of Satan [will be led and energized by Satan] with all power and lying wonders [in imitation of Jesus Christ], and with all deceivableness of unrighteousness in them that perish . . ." (II Thess. 2:9-10). Our Lord's warnings concerning the impostors of those days are most emphatic, as found in Matthew 24:2-5, 11, 24-25.

3. Satan has a kingdom of evil spirits. "And Jesus knew their thoughts, and said unto them, Every kingdom divided against itself is brought to desolation; and every city or house divided against itself shall not stand: And if Satan cast out Satan, he is divided against himself; how then shall *his kingdom* stand?" (Matt. 12:25-26).

Satan has a whole kingdom of evil spirits or demons. This was revealed by our Lord when the Pharisees spread the word that Jesus was casting out demons by the power of, and in the name of Beelzebub, the prince of the demons. While denying that he was in any way working in agreement with him, Jesus acknowledged that Satan did have a kingdom. From this revelation we may rightly conclude that Satan as king of that kingdom rules over his subjects, that they serve him, and that he uses them to carry out his schemes. While reserving the special study of demons to a later chapter, I call the reader's attention here to the admonition of the following Scripture verses: "Put on the whole armour of God, that ye may be able to stand against the wiles of the devil. For we wrestle not against flesh and blood, but against principalities, against powers, against the rulers of the darkness of this world, against spiritual wickedness in high places" (Eph. 6:11-12).

4. Satan's fatherhood. "Why do ye not understand my speech? even because ye cannot hear my word. Ye are of your father the devil, and the lusts of your father ye will do . . ." (John 8:43-44).

This description of Satan by our Lord is both shocking and sobering. In his work *The Teaching of Christ,* G. Campbell Morgan pointed out that the title "father" as Jesus used it here does not refer to origin of life, "but suggests care, watchfulness, attention; and the terrible thought of this passage therefore is that these men were under the care, the watchfulness, the attention of the devil . . . for the revelation of Scripture is that of the appalling persistence with which the devil will encompass the ruin of a soul, and the wreckage of society."

Someone has said that "all nature abhors a vacuum." This is true even in the realm of the spiritual. Wherever people refuse to make room in their lives for God as their Father, they will be taken over by the devil who will watch over them and fill their lives with his desires.

Satan watches over the unsaved as their father to protect them from the grace of God. The reason those antagonists of Christ did not understand His teaching was that they did not hear Him. Their spiritual ability to hear was shut off by the devil. They were yielded to him and did his bidding, his "lusts," or desires. Their hearts and minds were closed to the truth, and they carried out the desires of Satan who watched over them as a father. Some years later the Holy Spirit warned through the writing of the Apostle Paul: "But if our gospel be hid, it is hid to them that are lost: In whom the god of this world hath blinded the minds of them that believe not, lest the light of the glorious gospel of Christ, who is the image of God, should shine unto them" (II Cor. 4:3-4).

To those who are lost, the Gospel is "hid" or veiled. The reason why this veiling persists is that Satan has blinded their minds. It is an unalterable spiritual law that those who refuse the "Light of the world" will be blinded by the "god of this world," and darkness will envelop them. Satan watches over his own, and when there seems to be the least interest in spiritual things he will quickly bring into play every wile necessary to keep the person in unbelief.

To understand the full meaning of this spiritual blinding, we must remember that no unsaved person can understand or receive God's salvation on his own. "The natural man receiveth not the things of the Spirit of God: for they are foolishness unto him: neither can he know them, because they are spiritually discerned" (I Cor. 2:14). No human being can come to God for salvation without the divine enlightenment and enablement of the Holy Spirit. There are two great dangers related to this truth. The first is that Christian workers forget or ignore this truth and try to convert people. They do not depend completely on the Holy Spirit to convict and enlighten the hearer. The second danger is that when the Holy Spirit does bring conviction, does awaken the hearer to his need of Christ, the person closes his mind to the light. Satan will bring great pressure to bear to accomplish this closing of the mind. Having succeeded once, he will continue his blinding, and each rejection of Christ by the person involved makes Satan's work easier. Finally the person's heart is hardened in unbelief. Consider the solemn warning: "Wherefore as the Holy Ghost saith, To day if ye will hear his voice, harden not your hearts" (Heb. 3:7-8).

It might be added here that the devil has many blindfolds handy for his work, such as: the inconsistencies of professing Christians; the many divisions in Christianity and their disagreements on different doctrines; the (supposed) contradictions in the Bible; the (supposed) contradictions between Biblical facts and science. These are a few of Satan's favorite ideas which he uses to blind people's minds against the truth of the Gospel.

"Ye are of your father the devil." Having the devil for a father to direct your life—what a dreadful thought! I trust that the reader will be moved as I was moved by the reading of a sentence written by Dr. Lewis Sperry Chafer. Referring to the statement of John: "And we know that we are of God, and the whole world lieth in wickedness" (I John 5:19), Mr. Chafer wrote in *Systematic Theology:* "It requires more understanding concerning angelic realities than human beings possess to comprehend the meaning of the word *keimai,* here translated "lieth," which implies a vital, if not organic union between the unsaved and Satan. Out of such a relationship no individual may hope to be released apart from divine deliverance."

5. Satan, the sifter of men. "And the Lord said, Simon, Simon, behold, Satan hath desired to have you, that he may sift you as wheat. But I have prayed for thee, that thy faith fail not: and when thou art converted [hast turned again], strengthen thy brethren" (Luke 22:31-32).

Here our Lord drew aside the curtain just a bit so that we might have a glimpse of Satan's evil work in the lives of the Lord's own. Jesus said that Satan had desired to have Peter. This must mean that Satan had asked for Peter, had in fact demanded to have him, as the Greek indicates. Of whom did he demand to have Peter? The only answer to that can be that he demanded him of God. He wanted to have Peter so he could sift him like people in those days sifted or winnowed wheat. Satan wanted permission to put him through a complete test. This revelation sheds some light on Satan's suggestion millenniums earlier that if Job were turned over to him he would soon prove to God that the man was a hypocrite. Satan's request to try Job was granted, so this request to sift Peter was also granted.

Always, in the sifting of wheat, the purpose is to get rid of the worthless chaff and to collect the pure grain of wheat for useful food. But Satan sifts to get rid of the wheat and to collect the chaff for his evil purpose.

Is not this a frightening look behind the curtain? Satan asking for a person so he could sift him! His request being granted, and Peter ending up denying his Lord and Saviour! Cursing! We are inclined to ask: "Lord, what is going on? Do You know what You are doing?" But that is how it was, and we can be sure that Peter was not the first nor the last to be sifted by the devil.

Frightening as the picture appears, the results of that sifting are pure victories for the Lord's side. And when we look the second time, our hearts are filled with wonder and praise, and with renewed confidence in the Lord. In the first place, the situation also reveals to us the tender care and concern of the Lord for His own. "I have prayed for thee," said Jesus to Peter. When we need Him most, Jesus is the nearest to us. He knows, and He cares. "And when you have returned to me" (Twentieth Century Translation), "strengthen thy brethren." The whole scheme backfired on Satan. He was looking for chaff and there was plenty of that in Peter. This had to be removed before the Lord could trust him as the early leader of the whole movement of God's grace among mankind. There was the chaff of pride in Peter, along with the chaff of self-confidence which bordered on arrogance and boasting. There was also the chaff of impatience and rashness. All of this was sifted out of Peter and he came back to the Lord a different man. The Lord used Satan to sift Peter in the preparation of that apostle for the great work of the future. After the testing, Peter had great sympathy and patience with others who, like him, had failed in the sifting.

While meditating on these things, an interesting contrast came to my attention concerning the two apostles, Judas and Peter, and how they acted after Satan was through with them. Both had been used of the devil to hurt the Lord. Both went out, filled with sorrow over what they had done. But there the similarity ends. Judas "departed, and went and hanged himself" (Matt. 27:5). Peter "went out, and wept bitterly" (Matt. 26:75). The difference was that Judas was unsaved. When he had served the purpose of Satan, that murderer not only left him to despair, but blinded him to the fact that it still was not too late to throw himself upon the mercy of Christ. That is just like the devil! Peter was a saved man who really loved his Lord and with true repentance wept over his sin. The Lord did not leave him to despair. But with tender love He sent word on Resurrection morning through the angel: "Go your way, tell his disciples and Peter that he goeth before you into Galilee: there shall ye see him" (Mark 16:7). Can you imagine how sweet that "and Peter" must have sounded to the apostle on that eventful day? He soon was fully restored to fellowship by his Lord.

With the devil around—how wonderful to be on the Lord's side!

CHAPTER SEVEN

The Devil at Work in the Church

THE CHAPTER OUTLINED:

   I. Destruction of the Church through Persecution
      1. Our Lord forewarned His followers of coming persecution
      2. As soon as the Church was born, open persecution began . . .
      3. Persecution by Gentile powers was soon to follow

   II. Perversion of the Message of the Church through False Doctrine
      1. False teachings are inspired by Satan
      2. Satan's most effective counterfeit is Legalism . . .

   III. Paralyzing the Church through Compromise with the World
      1. The Word . . . teaches that the Church . . . be separated . . .
      2. Satan tries to get the Church to compromise with the world

   IV. Embarrassing the Church through Strife and Division

SUGGESTED BACKGROUND DEVOTIONAL READING

Monday—The Church with a Leaky Heart (Rev. 2:1-7)

Tuesday—The Devil Is Responsible for Persecution (Rev. 2:8-11)

Wednesday—The Doctrine of Balaam in the Church (Rev. 2:12-17)

Thursday—Compromise in the Church (Rev. 2:18-29)

Friday—A Living Corpse? (Rev. 3:1-6)

Saturday—The Church of the Open Door (Rev. 3:7-13)

Sunday—Lukewarmness in the Church (Rev. 3:14-21)

"And I say also unto thee, That thou art Peter, and upon this rock I will build my church; and the gates of hell *[hades]* shall not prevail against it" (Matt. 16:18).

Simon Peter had just declared that he believed Jesus to be the Son of God, the Christ whom God had sent to be the Saviour. This confession pleased Jesus greatly, and He recognized it as the work of God. He then announced the divine plan of building His Church upon the foundation of the truth which Peter had confessed and added the prediction that even the gates of hell would not be able to defeat it.

The word "Church" *(Ekklesia)* is used to describe different things. In the Bible it is never used of a church building as we use it today. Its primary usage is to describe the body of Christ which is made up of all born-again souls who share His life and nature, from Pentecost to His Second Coming. It is also used of local congregations of people who are organized to carry on the Lord's task for the Church. Such a local church may have in it both saved and unsaved members. The inspired writers of the New Testament viewed the local church or congregation as a miniature of the whole body of Christians. This fact gives us a third meaning of the Church, that of the whole mixed multitude of saved and unsaved church members who constitute the organized Church in the world at any given time. This is the Church that the world sees, which also is known as "Christendom."

God's purpose for the Church in this age is to evangelize all the world. The Church is to preach the Gospel and bear witness to Christ her Saviour and Lord. As people respond and receive Christ by faith, they are added to the true Church. Thus God is calling out of this world a people for His name.

The devil is 100 percent opposed to God's work of saving man from sin. Since God is working through the Church, Satan carries on a constant campaign of destroying, hindering and undermining the effectiveness of the Church in her God-appointed task. In this unrelenting opposition Satan uses all the powers at his disposal in the world, and all his secret agents within the Church, to try and defeat her. Our Lord implied that He foresaw Satan's opposition against the Church when He predicted that "the gates of hell shall not prevail against it" (Matt. 16:18). It is interesting to compare the different renderings by the translators of the New Testament. The following are of special note: "The powers of death shall not subdue it" (Goodspeed). "The powers of death shall never overpower it" (New English Bible). "The powers of the underworld shall never over-throw it" (Williams). "The might of Hades shall not triumph over it" (Weymouth).

The "gates of hell" are the powers of evil spirits who are under the control of Satan. They seek to destroy the true Church, but Christ is calling her to be His very own, and He never fails. The Church has been attacked, undermined, hindered, divided, and weakened, but she has not been destroyed. There were times through the dark centuries of the Middle Ages when her testimony seemed almost gone, but the Lord always had His own remnant who held aloft the Light of the Lord. And after almost 2,000 years of hell's onslaught, the Church is still very much alive in spite of all the devices Satan has used against her.

As we study the New Testament and the history of the Church through the past 19 centuries, we discover that Satan in his warfare has been using four different tactics in his overall strategy. These basic tactics are:

Destruction of the Church through Persecution
Perversion of the Message of the Church through False Doctrine
Paralyzing the Church through Compromise with the World
Embarrassing the Church through Strife and Division

These tactics are very different one from the other. The first and the third are complete opposites. They are all employed by Satan today, but they are not new, for they were all used by him in the first 40 years of the existence of the Church. He will use the one that will do the most damage and is the most likely to succeed at any place in the world where the true Church is effectively bringing souls in contact with Jesus Christ.

I. Destruction of the Church through Persecution

"Fear none of those things which thou shalt suffer: behold, *the devil shall cast some of you into prison,* that ye may be tried; and ye shall have tribulation ten days: be thou faithful unto death, and I will give thee the crown of life" (Rev. 2:10).

These words of our Lord were addressed to the church at Smyrna. The Book of Acts reports many vicious endeavors by the ruling powers in Jerusalem to stop believers there from promoting the Gospel. The Church was outlawed, and those who continued to speak up for Christ were ar-rested, imprisoned, often beaten and tortured, and sometimes killed. All of this is well known, but what is often overlooked is the fact that behind these persecutions is Satan who seeks to destroy the Church. He is the spiritual leader of this world and uses the powers of government to forbid the preaching of the Gospel wherever he can.

1. Our Lord forewarned His followers of coming persecution. ". . . but because ye are not of the world, but I have chosen you out of the world, therefore the world hateth you. Remember the word that I have said unto you, The servant is not greater than his lord. If they have persecuted me, they will also persecute you" (John 15:19-20). "These things have I spoken unto you, that ye should not be offended. They shall put you out of the synagogues: yea, the time cometh, that whosoever killeth you will think that he doeth God service" (John 16:1-2). "These things I have spoken unto you, that in me ye might have peace. In the world ye shall have tribulation: but be of good cheer: I have overcome the world" (John 16:33).

These warnings were given the disciples on the night before the crucifixion. It is obvious that our Lord wanted them to remember what He had told them, lest they be shocked when the mighty storm of hatred and violence would come down on them.

2. As soon as the Church was born, open persecution began through the Jewish leaders. Peter and John were arrested a few days after Pentecost (Acts 4:1-3). A few days later the apostles were arrested on the order of the High Priest (Acts 5:17-18), and the next day the first beating was administered to them (Acts 5:40-41).

The persecution of the early Christians erupted into full fury when Stephen was stoned to death after a sort of trial before the Council, which was presided over by the High Priest (Acts 6:8-15; 7:1, 54-60). The stoning of Stephen precipitated an all-out campaign by the Jewish authorities to silence the young Church once and for all. The sacred record records it in a few terse sentences. "And Saul was consenting unto his [Stephen's] death. And at that time there was a great persecution against the church which was at Jerusalem; and they were all scattered abroad throughout the regions of Judaea and Samaria, except the apostles. . . . As for Saul, he made havoc of the church, entering into every house, and haling men and women committed them to prison" (Acts 8:1, 3). "And Saul, yet breathing out threatenings and slaughter against the disciples of the Lord . . ." (Acts 9:1).

Soon the persecution took on a more authoritative character when King Herod officially took a hand in putting Christians to death. "Now about that time Herod the king stretched forth his hands to vex certain of the church. And he killed James the brother of John with the sword. And because he saw that it pleased the Jews, he proceeded further to take Peter also" (Acts 12:1-3).

3. Persecution by Gentile powers was soon to follow. For the first 30 years the persecution of the Church was almost entirely the work of the Jews against Jewish Christians, under the leadership of the Sanhedrin, the assembly of men who held a combination of religious and political authority over the Jews. During those early days there was no official antagonism against the Church from the government of Rome. There were local outbreaks of Gentile opposition against Christians such as Paul and his companions experienced in almost every city where they preached the Gospel. That even the churches which had been established in Europe were subjected to open persecution can be observed from reading Paul's first letter to the church at Thessalonica (cf. I Thess. 2:14-16).

The most terrible persecution of the Church began in the year A.D. 64, when the Roman Empire officially entered the battle and was used of Satan in a ruthless struggle to obliterate the Christian faith from the earth. This open warfare began with Nero, following the terrible fire of Rome. The news leaked out that Nero had set the fire himself, and when he was unable to convince the populace of his innocence, he accused the Christians of having set the city on fire. I believe both Peter and Paul speak of that persecution in their letters (cf. I Peter 4:12-19; II Tim. 4:6).

The persecution was carried on under the public banner of a revival of the old national religions of Rome, which centered around emperor worship. Believers were brought into court and questioned as to whether they were Christians. If they admitted they were, they were ordered to renounce their allegiance to Christ by repeating a prepared "invocation of the gods," and by offering wine or incense on the statue of the emperor. Those who did not comply were "punished." If they were Roman citizens, their punishment usually was death by being beheaded with the sword. Those who did not hold Roman citizenship were subjected to all manner of torture and death by such cruel methods as crucifixion, burning, or being thrown into an arena with wild beasts after having first been clothed in animal skins.

For over 200 years such persecutions raged against the Church. Believers went underground for worship and to bury their dead, as the hundreds of miles of catacombs beneath ancient Rome testify to this day. It is impossible to say how many thousands of Christians lost their lives. The second great persecution under the Emperor Domitian (A.D. 95) alone is supposed to have claimed the lives of 40,000 believers. There were ten major persecutions, and for 240 years it was a crime against the state to be a Christian—and for this crime there was no forgiveness. Anyone who would follow Christ had to be prepared to pay for it at any moment with the loss of liberty and life.

The persecution of the Church by Rome ended officially in A.D. 313, when the Emperor Constantine issued the "Edict of Milan," a declaration which promised freedom of belief to the individual. Thus ended an era of ruthless and official suppression by the strongest world power. Satan, through Rome, had done his worst, and had failed miserably. Persecutions, instead of exterminating the Church as had been expected, served actually to purify the Church and hastened the spreading of the Gospel.

Although Satan changed tactics when that persecution failed, it did not mean that he abandoned it altogether. He has continued to use it wherever he has found a world power willing to do his work. After that first all-out endeavor, his favored method has been to use the "Church" to persecute true believers in the name of the Christian faith (so-called). Nor is the world today without its persecutions. There are many silent sufferers among the scattered believers in areas ruled by Communism (China, Russia, North Korea, North Vietnam, Eastern Europe). In some areas of Africa believers are suffering severe persecution under the old banner of revival of nationalism. Some have suffered from persecution of the "Church" in such lands as Colombia and Spain, severe a few years ago, but dormant while this is being written. The devil still uses the weapon of persecution cunningly, wherever he finds it possible and useful.

II. Perversion of the Message of the Church through False Doctrine

The calling of the Church is to preach the Gospel in all the world. This Gospel is the good news of God's salvation for man through Jesus Christ. It is the story of what God has done through Christ to make this salvation possible. This is the message that God has promised to bless. In the words of the Apostle Paul: ". . . it is the power of God unto salvation . . ." (Rom. 1:16). Since it is Satan's obsession to keep man from being saved from his sin, we are not surprised that he should concentrate on having that message changed in order to make it ineffective. This is exactly what he has tried to do from the very beginning of the Church, and with this tactic he has been far more successful than with his attack through persecution.

1. False teachings are inspired by Satan. Of course, men are the instruments through whom Satan presents all his false doctrines. They are called by various titles in the Word of God, such as: "False prophets . . . in sheep's clothing" (Matt. 7:15); "False apostles" (II Cor. 11:13); "False teachers . . . who . . . bring in damnable [destructive] heresies. . . . [who] with feigned words make merchandise of you [sell you out] . . ." (II Peter 2:1-3). While men and women are the agents, the real source of these destructive teachings is Satan. This is clearly indicated by the inspired writers as well as by our Lord himself. The Apostle Paul declared that the false apostles and deceitful workers who appear as the apostles of Christ and as ministers of righteousness, are actually *the ministers of Satan* (II Cor. 11:13-15). Years later, Paul wrote to Timothy: "Now the Spirit speaketh expressly, that in the latter times some shall depart from the faith, giving heed to seducing spirits, and *doctrines of devils*; speaking lies in hypocrisy . . ." (I Tim. 4:1-2). A very interesting translation of the last phrase is found in The Living Bible which reads: "These teachers will tell lies with straight faces."

In His letter to the Church at Thyatira our Lord accused that congregation of tolerating "that woman Jezebel, which calleth herself a prophetess, to teach and to seduce my servants to commit fornication, and to eat things sacrificed to idols" (Rev. 2:20). The Jezebel of the Old Testament was the wicked wife of King Ahab of Israel who brought Baal worship to that land and mixed it with Jehovah worship. The "fornication" introduced in Thyatira by "this Jezebel of a woman" (Moffatt), speaks of spiritual fornication which is the mixing of error with the truth. These errors were taught by a woman who posed as a prophetess, but who was an instrument of Satan. After promising severe judgment unless there was a genuine repentance, the Lord addressed those who had remained faithful with: "As many as have not this doctrine, and which have not known *the depths of Satan*. . . ." The "depths of Satan" refer to "the deep mysteries (as they are called) which Satan offers" (Knox Translation). This identifies Satan as the real source of the spiritual fornication.

John, the apostle of love, was moved by the Holy Spirit to issue this solemn warning: "Beloved, believe not every spirit, but try the spirits whether they are of God: because many false prophets are gone out into the world" (I John 4:1). John speaks of spirits and false prophets as though they were the same. This is so because the false teachers are inspired by evil spirits who are in the employ of Satan.

The false doctrines by which Satan has robbed the Church of much of her effectiveness are many and varied. There is not room in this study to examine them. Their general purpose is to detract in some way from the Person and work of the Son of God as the only basis of man's salvation from sin. Some of the false doctrines are aimed at denying the full deity of Jesus Christ as in so-called Modernism and in the teaching of Jehovah's Witnesses today. Much of false doctrine is concentrated on denying the absolute necessity of man's spiritual regeneration as, for example, in the popular teaching of the Universal Fatherhood of God and the Universal Brotherhood of Man. Sometimes the false teachings do their damage by simply stressing one aspect of the work of the Church while completely neglecting the spiritual need of man, as represented today by the well-named "Social Gospel."

2. Satan's most effective counterfeit is Legalism—salvation by Christ, plus something else. The oldest and most successful deception which Satan has sold to the Church is the denial of justification by grace alone. It has been most successful because it has much truth in it and because it appeals to human pride, and therefore is most reasonable to the natural man. This was the first false doctrine that plagued the Early Church and which precipitated the first Church Council in Jerusalem (Acts 15). A number of teachers were busy in the Early Church insisting that man must keep the Law of Moses to be saved. They demanded that Gentiles, before they could be saved, had to be circumcised and keep the Law the same as Jews (cf. Acts 15:1, 5).

Although the Church officially settled the controversy at that time, it has never died completely, and the battle has to be fought again in every generation. The Apostle Paul was dogged in his travels by these false teachers. He seemed to understand the issue most clearly and fought hardest against the heresy. He had seen it swallow up the whole Galatian churches until those who had been saved by the grace of God were so overpowered by the heresy that they tried to be sanctified by their own works. In great sorrow and exasperation he wrote: "I marvel that ye are so soon removed from him that called you into the grace of Christ unto another gospel: Which is not another; but there be some that trouble you, and would pervert the gospel of Christ. But though we, or an angel from heaven, preach any other gospel unto you than that which we have preached unto you, let him be accursed" (Gal. 1:6-8). "O FOOLISH Galatians, who hath bewitched you, that ye should not obey the truth, before whose eyes Jesus Christ hath been evidently set forth, crucified among you? . . . Are ye so foolish? having begun in the Spirit, are ye now made perfect by the flesh?" (Gal. 3:1, 3).

From that day to this, the adding something to or the substituting something for the grace of God as the basis of man's salvation, has been the number one counterfeit of Satan in the Church. That which is added and that which is substituted may change with the times, but the intent and result is ever the same. It insults God and robs the one who heeds it, at least of peace and assurance, if not of salvation itself. That which is added to, or substituted for the grace of God as a basis of salvation, may be baptism, good works, sacraments, door-to-door witnessing, church membership, mortification of the flesh, confession, repentance, commandment keeping, prayer, piety, and a great number of other human endeavors. No matter what it is that is added or substituted, it is a denial of one of the most fundamental doctrines of the Word of God: namely, that man is justified (declared to be, and accepted as righteous by God) *through grace alone,* made possible through the shed blood of the Son of God, and received by faith. Having grown up in a church that teaches the mixture of Christ plus your good works and commandment keeping as the means of saving a person from sin, I believe that a majority of church members living today are duped by Satan in holding that view. Perhaps some of them are saved (I know that God is very gracious and that He "delighteth in mercy"), but they have neither peace nor assurance, and are hoping for the best. The devil is a sneak.

III. Paralyzing the Church through Compromise with the World

The Word of God needs to be believed to be effective for salvation. That is why Satan tries to slip in his counterfeit doctrines.

The Word of God needs to be lived by those who are saved, to make it believable to the unsaved. Therefore, Satan tries to draw the Church away from a walk with God to follow the ways of the world.

1. The Word of God teaches that the Church is to be separated from the world. The Church is a body of people who are called out of the world. They are not of the world (John 15:18-19; 17:14). Believers are not to be "conformed to this world: but be . . . transformed . . ." and thus prove (demonstrate) "what is that good, and acceptable, and perfect will of

God" (Rom. 12:2). The Spirit warned the Church: "Know ye not that the friendship of the world is enmity with God? whosoever therefore will be the friends of the world is the enemy of God" (James 4:4). John thus exhorted believers: "Love not the world, neither the things that are in the world. If any man love the world, the love of the Father is not in him" (I John 2:15).

It is impossible to follow the Lord and the world at the same time. Years ago it was my privilege to listen to Dr. Harry Rimmer expound the Word of God in his unique and convincing manner. I remember an illustration he used to demonstrate the impossibility of the Church or the individual believer following the Lord and the world at the same time, which went somewhat like this: "I have seen some great riders in my days. I remember seeing a young lady riding two horses at the same time in a circus tent. She had one foot on the back of each horse as they trotted side by side around the ring. But I have never seen nor ever heard of a rider who could ride two horses at the same time when they were going in opposite directions. The Lord and the world are going in opposite directions."

The Church is to be in the world but is not of the world. She is like a ship in the ocean, a very useful and remarkable means of transportation. When the ocean gets into the ship—then there is disaster and the ship is lost and becomes useless. When the world gets into the Church, there is spiritual disaster and she loses her usefulness.

2. Satan tries to get the Church to compromise with the world. In the letter to the Church at Pergamos the Lord diagnosed the situation there as follows: "I know thy works, and where thou dwellest, even *where Satan's seat is.* . . . But I have a few things against thee, because thou hast there them that hold the doctrine of Balaam, who taught Balac to cast a stumblingblock before the children of Israel, to eat things sacrificed unto idols, and to commit fornication" (Rev. 2:13-14).

Balaam was a prophet whom King Balac hired to put a curse on Israel. When the Lord would not permit this, Balaam tried to figure out some other way to earn his fee. He then told Balac that he could defeat Israel by acting friendly and by inviting the men of Israel into his camp so that they would get mixed up with the women of Moab. This mixing of Israel with the world would weaken the nation spiritually and Balac would be able to defeat it. Balaam tried to please both God and Balac and profit from both.

This is one of Satan's methods with which he hopes to defeat the

Church. When his all-out persecution of the Church by the world failed, he suddenly changed tactics and invited the Church to enter the world. Within a few generations the Church and the world were one; joined in politics, in finances, in crime, even in bloody wars. Satan almost prevailed, but the Lord kept for himself a remnant, a minority, until the Reformation came, followed later by a new breath of fresh air and a resurgence of spiritual power that sent missionaries to the far places of the earth to tell the old, old story of Jesus and His love.

This mixing of the world and the Church is still one of Satan's favored strategies. His present ambition seems to be to bring all churches and cults together into one great super church which will be apostate and ready for Satan's false christ to use in helping him to become the world dictator. This great religious monstrosity is called "the great whore," and "mother of harlots" by the Lord, and is described in chapters 17 and 18 of the Book of the Revelation.

IV. Embarrassing the Church through Strife and Division

The greatest burden of our Lord's high priestly prayer on the night before His death was for the spiritual unity and harmony of His people in order that the world might believe on Him. Repeatedly He prayed that "they might be one" (John 17:11, 21-23). The devil knows that a congregation of people who love the Lord and who walk together in Spirit-led love and harmony, is unbeatable. He therefore delights in stirring up strife and division, making sure that the world hears about it, in order to silence the testimony of that people.

When the Early Church grew rapidly, Satan tried to weaken it by starting a "murmuring of the Grecians against the Hebrews" (Acts 6:1). The "Hebrews" were the native sons of Palestine. The "Grecians" were Jews born in other parts of the world whose lives had been affected by Greek culture. Because of the air of superiority displayed by the Hebrews, there was a long-standing animosity between the two groups. Now they were both saved and lived together in Christian love and harmony. This was wonderful! However, the old nature was still capable of renewing old prejudices. All it needed was a little priming, and at this business Satan is a past master. Knowing human nature well, he planted a small seed of suspicion in the minds of some Grecians and let it germinate. Soon there was a little whisper, which snowballed into dangerous murmuring. "The Hebrews are not playing fair . . . isn't that just like them? . . . we should have expected it!" The goodwill and testimony seemed to vanish. A split seemed inevitable. Such a tragedy was prevented when the Holy Spirit was allowed to take over in a business meeting.

This was not the last time Satan tried to cause strife and division in a local church. Contention even split up the greatest missionary team (Acts 15:36-39). Strife, caused by suspicion, envy, or "vainglory" is one of the devices of Satan by which he would ruin the testimony of the local church, and the work of missionaries. Let us beware of this trap, for it is a clever one. Let us take seriously the warning of the apostle: "Let nothing be done through strife or vainglory; but in lowliness of mind let each esteem other better than themselves" (Phil. 2:3). One of Satan's great victories against the testimony of a congregation was accomplished through causing strife and division. This fact we gather from Paul's sad reproof to the Corinthians: "For it hath been declared unto me of you, my brethren . . . that there are contentions among you. Now this I say, that every one of you saith, I am of Paul; and I of Apollos; and I of Cephas; and I of Christ" (I Cor. 1:11-12).

The church in Corinth was caught in one of Satan's oldest traps, that of strife and division over human leaders. There is no evidence that those leaders were responsible, but Satan had managed to cause the splits somehow. In our day so many congregations have split in a disgraceful manner because their leader was humbly willing to have the people take sides over him.

Of course, there are times when division is good for an enlarged ministry, and this can be accomplished in a spirit of love to the glory of God. There are also times when the honor of the Lord's name calls for a leader to take a stand, even if it should result in a division. But there are divisions of congregations that are not of the Lord. They are caused by Satan who uses human pride, suspicion and selfishness to accomplish his purpose. If only we would understand that Satan is forever seeking to discredit the local church to keep her from drawing souls to Christ! If only we would remember in times of tension that soon the Chief Shepherd may appear, and we must give account to Him! If only we would let the Holy Spirit take over in our business meetings! "Behold, how good and how pleasant it is for brethren to dwell together in unity" (Ps. 133:1).

CHAPTER EIGHT

How To Defeat the Devil

THE CHAPTER OUTLINED:

   I. The Believer Is No Match for This Powerful Enemy

  II. Christ Is the Victory
     1. The basis of the believer's victory is . . work of Christ
     2. Satan has the power of death

 III. The Armor God Wants Us to Wear
     1. The Lord Jesus Christ, the only source of victory
     2. The believer's stand is to be "against . . . the devil"
     3. The armor which we are asked to wear is God's armor
     4. The first part of the armor is the girdle . . . of truth
     5. The breastplate of righteousness
     6. "And your feet shod with . . . the gospel of peace"
     7. "Taking the shield of faith, . . . ye shall be able to quench . . .
     8. "And take the helmet of salvation"
     9. "And the sword of the Spirit which is the word of God"

SUGGESTED BACKGROUND DEVOTIONAL READING

Monday—Victory "In the Name of the Lord" (I Sam. 17:38-50)

Tuesday—Victory "By the Blood of the Lamb" (Rev. 12:7-12)

Wednesday—Death Has Lost Its Sting (I Cor. 15:51-58)

Thursday—Hiding the Word in the Heart (Ps. 119:9-16)

Friday—The Messenger of Satan (II Cor. 12:7-10)

Saturday—"In Christ," No Condemnation (Rom. 8:1-10)

Sunday—"In Christ," No Separation (Rom. 8:31-39)

The study of Satan would not be complete without a consideration of the believer's part in the spiritual warfare that Satan carries on against God's plan for man. Satan is the sworn enemy of the person who has received the Lord Jesus into his life. This is so because Satan is the enemy of God, and the true believer has become a child of God and is a partaker of the spiritual life and nature of God.

One of the great surprises of new Christians is that they still find themselves bothered with temptations. Lustful and ugly thoughts, and even occasional doubts about God still come up in the mind. They expect to be free from them once they are born again, but soon discover otherwise. Sometimes temptations seem to increase with the gift of salvation. This can be quite unsettling to the new Christian, but in reality this is a source of assurance. The Word of God is plain and emphatic in warning believers of the intense warfare that Satan, assisted by his kingdom of evil spirits, carries on against them. We should expect this warfare, and when it comes we can take it as an added evidence that we are on the right road. Every personal worker should carefully explain this fact when instructing a new convert.

I. The Believer Is No Match for This Powerful Enemy

A brief consideration of what the Bible says about Satan's warfare against the believer turns up the following solemn warnings: "Put on the whole armour of God, that ye may be able to stand against the wiles of the devil" (Eph. 6:11). The devil's "wiles" are his clever schemes. Satan shoots "fiery darts" at us (v. 16).

Through his "devices" Satan seeks to get the advantage of the believer (II Cor. 2:11). Peter (who knew about it by experience) warned: ". . . the devil, as a roaring lion, walketh about, seeking whom he may devour" (I Peter 5:8).

The devil is "the accuser of our brethren . . . which accused them before our God day and night" (Rev. 12:10). Through false teaching he takes people "captive . . . at his will" (II Tim. 2:26). We are warned against falling into "the snare of the devil" (I Tim. 3:7).

Paul tells us that he was hindered in his work by Satan (I Thess. 2:18). The "thorn in the flesh" (a physical pain) which plagued Paul, was "a messenger of Satan" (II Cor. 12:7). Christ revealed that Satan has power to afflict people with physical ailments (cf. Luke 13:11-13, 16). The Holy Spirit revealed that Satan has the power of death (cf. Heb. 2:14), and that he inspires the persecution of believers (cf. Rev. 2:10).

As we look at this array of Satan's power and cunning, we may well be alarmed. We are hopelessly outclassed in a warfare with Satan and his host. This is exactly what our Lord wants us to see. Victory over Satan is possible for every believer, but not in our own strength. We are like young David facing Goliath. Putting on King Saul's armor, David knew he would be helpless against the giant. He put off man's armor and placed himself into God's hands; stepped out to meet the dreaded enemy of Israel, saying: "I come to thee in the name of the Lord of hosts" (I Sam. 17:45). Every child in Sunday School knows the story of the victory that resulted, but the story of that unusual battle and victory is not in the Bible for the sake of dramatics. It is there to show us what God will do if we trust Him and lean upon Him instead of trusting in our own strength or skill. This fact is the background of the believer's victory over Satan.

II. Christ Is the Victory

While meditating on God's provision for the believer's victory over the many traps of Satan, the words of Martin Luther came to mind. It is obvious that he understood the subject very well.

> For still our ancient foe
> Doth seek to work us woe;
> His craft and power are great,
> And armed with cruel hate,
> On earth is not his equal.

> Did we in our own strength confide,
> Our striving would be losing;
> Were not the right Man on our side,
> The Man of God's own choosing.
> Dost ask who that may be?
> Christ Jesus, it is He;
> Lord Sabaoth is His name;
> From age to age the same;
> And He must win the battle.

> And though this world with devils filled,
> Should threaten to undo us;
> We will not fear, for God hath willed
> His truth to triumph through us.

The prince of darkness grim
We tremble not for him;
His rage we can endure,
For lo! his doom is sure,
One little word shall fell him.

What are the provisions that God has made for the believer's victory over Satan? What is it that the believer must do to take full advantage of those provisions?

1. The basis of the believer's victory is in the redemptive work of Christ. "And they overcame him [Satan] *by the blood of the Lamb,* and by the word of their testimony" (Rev. 12:11).

"For this purpose the Son of God was manifested, that he might destroy the works of the devil" (I John 3:8).

"Forasmuch then as the children are partakers of flesh and blood, he also himself likewise took part of the same; that through death he might destroy him that had the power of death, that is, the devil; and deliver them who through fear of death were all their lifetime subject to bondage" (Heb. 2:14-15).

To overcome Satan we must recognize that he has been defeated by Christ through His atoning death and consequent resurrection, and that our victory is only in Christ. Many defeated believers make the mistake of asking the Lord to help them overcome the devil. This will not do at all. We are not saved by asking the Lord to help us save ourselves. Christ *is* our Saviour, the only one who can save us. Even so the Lord *is* our victory, and there is no other. Even the Archangel Michael would not think of fighting Satan, but asked the Lord to take care of the adversary (Jude 9).

2. Satan has the power of death (cf. Heb. 2:14-15). I doubt if anyone understands all that is involved in this statement that Jesus became a human being so "that through death he might destroy him that had the power of death, that is, the devil" (v. 14). It is true that indirectly Satan causes many deaths, for "he is a murderer from the beginning" (John 8:44). He destroys human lives through wars, through the hatreds of men, through the power of alcohol, and even through the forces of nature. But there is more here than that, for wars and hatreds and drunkenness continue to kill and destroy lives.

What is involved in Satan's power of death? How did Christ destroy Satan in this power? Death is the result of sin, being part of the judgment of God upon man's rebellion against Him. "The wages of sin is death" (Rom. 6:23). "The soul that sinneth, it shall die" (Ezek. 18:4). Death is Satan's realm, where he holds sway. When Jesus Christ as the Second Adam, being sinless himself, gave His life for man's sin, He accomplished the redemption of man from sin and its results. Through Christ's substitutionary death, Satan lost his claim on every human being who is joined to Christ by faith. When a person is saved, he is placed under the blood of Christ and becomes part of Christ, being fully identified with Him in His death, resurrection, and future glory.

In the substitutionary death of Christ, death itself is annulled or counteracted because His death provided a wonderful remedy for death. The remedy for spiritual death is the new birth with its new life from God. The remedy for physical death is the resurrection and transformation into the likeness of our Redeemer. All this is part of God's gift of salvation. And now death has lost its dread for the believer, for it is only the stepping stone or door into the presence of the Lord. Now we can confidently sing and shout: "O death, where is thy sting? O grave, where is thy victory? The sting of death is sin, and the strength of sin is the law. But thanks be to God, which giveth *us the victory through our Lord Jesus Christ*" (I Cor. 15:55-57).

The word that is translated "destroy" in Hebrews 2:14 is the interesting Greek word *katargeo* which never carries the idea of annihilation, but means undoing, annulling, or making powerless. This word is used to describe the fact that death dissolves (katargeo) the bond of marriage, freeing the living party to marry again. "For the woman which hath an husband is bound by the law to her husband as long as he liveth; but if the husband be dead, she is loosed from the law of her husband" (Rom. 7:2). Here the word is translated "is loosed." In Romans 4:14 the same word is used to give expression to Israel making God's promises "of none effect," through legalism; for the promises are to be received by faith. They "katargeo" God's promises, they make them powerless because they do not come to God in faith.

Putting it all together we understand that even as Israel neutralized God's promises, and even as the bond of marriage is dissolved by death for the widow or widower, so Satan with his power of death has been neutralized, has been put out of business, has been rendered powerless by the substitutionary death of the Son of God. And, in Christ the believer has the possibility of complete victory over Satan no matter how loud

Satan may shout or threaten. He has no power against us unless we grant it to him. He is a foe, but a defeated one.

The late Dr. Donald Grey Barnhouse used an illustration which I want to relate word for word. He is here picturing the actual position of the believer in relation to Satan and to sin. Regarding the meaning of the Greek word *katargeo,* Dr. Barnhouse, in *God's Freedom,* wrote:

"Christ died, Paul says, in order that through His death 'he might destroy him that had the power of death, that is, the devil' (Heb. 2:14). We have only to look around us to know that Satan still exists. He has not been put out of existence, nor has he been rendered inoperative. But the work of Christ has established principles whereby Satan can be overcome day by day. In this sense the word must be used in connection with our old devilish nature. Like Satan, it exists and is active, but the principles for overcoming it are already established. God has not left us without power; in His sight Satan and our old nature are rendered powerless when we avail ourselves of what God has given us. Imagine an unarmed American soldier on Guadalcanal standing helpless before a rifle aimed by the enemy. That is our position before Christ died for us . . . But when Christ died, the rifle was knocked from the hands of our captor. Now he must stand with hands raised, while the rifle points at him. He will tell us that our rifle is not loaded, that the bayonet is papier-mache. He will challenge us to lay it aside and fight him with judo, of which he is a master. But when we realize that the weapon of triumph has been put into our hands, that our captor is now our prisoner, we can have practical victory over sin."

Satan has been defeated. He has been stripped of his power by the Son of God. The devil's threats are empty. Through our Lord's substitutionary death He redeemed man from Satan's domain. And when a person chooses Christ as his Saviour and Lord of life, Satan has no more claim or power over him. By faith the believer is in Christ Jesus and is partaker of Christ's victory. So when Satan comes (and come he will), either to tempt, to accuse, or to attack, we must take our stand upon the shed blood of Christ, for therein lies Satan's defeat.

III. The Armor God Wants Us to Wear

The greatest passage dealing with the believer's victory over Satan is found in Paul's letter to the Ephesians, chapter 6, verses 10-17. In these verses it is all spelled out—the believer's only base of victory, the enemy's great cunning, and the practical equipment which God has provided for a day-by-day carrying out of this victory. Note the metaphor of a soldier's armor.

1. The Lord Jesus Christ, the only source of victory. "Finally, my brethren, *be strong in the Lord,* and in the power of his might" (Eph. 6:10). Paul begins his presentation of God's blueprint for victory over Satan by directing us to the only source of victory which is the Person of the Lord Jesus Christ. The believer is not encouraged to flex his muscles and be strong, but to be strong in the Lord and in His almighty power. This is the most important statement of the whole passage, and until we fully recognize the principle that Christ is our victory, we will be defeated before we start.

2. The believer's stand is to be "against the wiles of the devil" (Eph. 6:11). The Lord expects His people to stand, not to fall. He has provided a full armor of protection. The "wiles" of the devil point to his cunning and deceptive schemes or tricks by which he tries to bring about the believer's fall. He is full of tricks. He centers his attack on our weakest parts. He often makes his appeal through the natural appetites of the physical body, such as the desire for food—". . . command that these stones be made bread" (Matt. 4:3); or the natural desire of sex. He tries to make what is ugly look beautiful, and presents what is wrong as being right. He attacks through weakness and strain, through sickness and pain. He has a whole bag full of tricks. He can make an illicit relationship seem to be something holy instead of the abomination that it is in the sight of the Lord.

Satan also makes his approach through the mind. There, too, he seeks out our weakest point and works on that, whether it be pride, ambition, envy, the desire to shine, to get even, or feelings that get hurt easily. He also works on and through our lack of patience, and our fear of man. In sifting Simon Peter, Satan discovered that the apostle was afraid of what people might say about him. He soon ambushed Peter and brought him down into defeat (cf. Mark 14:66-72). He never forgot about that weak spot of Peter, and years later he worked the same trick again with some success (cf. Gal. 2:11-12). He was able to lead Peter into compromise because the apostle was "fearing them which were of the circumcision." He likes to work through a youth's fear of being left without a date or without a mate. He ever works through our inferiority complexes. Perhaps the most dangerous trick of Satan is to get a believer to acquire a feeling or an air of spiritual superiority.

3. The armor which we are asked to wear is God's armor (Eph. 6:11). God has provided it and so it is perfectly suited to its purpose. The metaphor is taken from the soldier's armor in the days when bow and arrow, sword and lance were the weapons of warfare. The armor was for protection. God's armor is to protect us against Satan's wiles and fiery darts. Our protection is not in our own strength or schemes, but in that which God has provided.

4. The first part of the armor is the girdle or belt of truth (Eph. 6:14). Jesus said, "I am . . . the truth" (John 14:6). When talking to His Father He said, ". . . thy word is truth" (John 17:17). We need a simple and clear grasp of the truth as revealed in the Word of God. In presenting the armor of God, Paul used the aorist participle four times, thus showing that the armor is to be put on before the believer is expected to stand. A more accurate translation would read: "Having girded our loins with truth . . . and having put on the breastplate of righteousness . . . and having shod our feet . . . having taken up the shield of faith." The significance of this is that the believer is expected to be prepared to stand; already having on the armor, not letting it hang in the armory, and then trying to dust it off for an emergency. The Psalmist said: "Thy word have I hid in mine heart, that I might not sin against thee" (Ps. 119:11). It is best to have God's Word in the heart by daily usage. You cannot always run to a concordance and look for the verse you need. Some people let the Bible fall open and use the verse which first attracts the eye as an answer to a problem. This is both foolish and presumptuous.

5. The breastplate of righteousness (Eph. 6:14). The breastplate was that part of the armor which protected the vital organs of the body, the heart and lungs. The heart is apt to condemn us until we have received the righteousness of God in Christ and know what this means. God's righteousness alone is wound-proof. This part of the armor is especially important when Satan comes with his accusations. He manages to rob many believers of joy and peace by reminding them of old sins and present shortcomings, filling their hearts with doubts and fears. The only way to overcome this form of attack is to be fully aware of, and to fully rely upon, the righteousness of God that is the believer's possession in Christ. "For he [God] hath made him [Christ] to be sin for us, who knew no sin; that we might be made the righteousness of God in him" (II Cor. 5:21). Satan's accusations will lose their power when we fully trust God's promise that "there is therefore now no condemnation to them which are in Christ Jesus . . ." (Rom. 8:1).

6. **"And your feet shod with the preparation of the gospel of peace"** (Eph. 6:15). The good news of peace is that Christ "is our peace" (Eph. 2:14). He has "made peace through the blood of his cross" (Col. 1:20). "Therefore being justified by faith, we have peace with God through our Lord Jesus Christ" (Rom. 5:1). This is the best footing for the believer's daily walk which is filled with all sorts of obstacles. "Put shoes on his feet," was the father's order when welcoming home the wandering son.

7. **"Taking the shield of faith, wherewith ye shall be able to quench all the fiery darts of the wicked"** (Eph. 6:16). The shield of the soldier was for warding off the missiles that came flying through the air. Satan puts plenty of fire into his missiles. They are aimed at the center of the believer's spiritual life. To quench them we need a simple, childlike faith in God and in His promises. I am of the conviction that what God wants most from His children is that they believe Him. That simple trust will extinguish Satan's most fiery dart.

8. **"And take the helmet of salvation"** (Eph. 6:17). The believer's helmet is also called "the hope of salvation" (I Thess. 5:8). I believe that the true meaning of this helmet of salvation has to do with the assurance of salvation. The "hope" of salvation has nothing to do with uncertainty, but is the certainty of knowing that the final goal of salvation is to be like Christ in glory. No one is "strong in the Lord and in the power of his might" who lacks assurance of personal salvation. The devil will pester the life out of a person who does not accept God's Word for his salvation.

9. **"And the sword of the Spirit which is the word of God"** (Eph. 6:17). This is the Spirit's sword which God has put into our hands. Its purpose is for both defense and offense. Man-made swords are useless in the believer's stand against the wiles of Satan. Our own arguments do not win spiritual battles. Our Lord used this sword (God's Word) to ward off every thrust of Satan in the wilderness.

Let us go back for a moment to the admonition with which the presentation of the armor is introduced: "Be strong in the Lord, and in the power of his might" (Eph. 6:10). There is victory for every believer. That victory is not in our striving and trying, but in Christ Jesus. Even the armor is His.

I am hoping that at this point the reader is asking: "What then is my responsibility?" The answer to this legitimate question is not to go out and face the enemy and do your best. Your responsibility and mine is to recognize the Lord Jesus as the victor, to trust Him by putting on the armor which He has provided. This is both faith and obedience. This is being "strong in the Lord, and in the power of *his* might." This is resisting the devil, "stedfast in the faith" (I Peter 5:9).

But you have already failed the Lord? Yes, and so had Abraham, Jacob, Samson, David, Peter, Thomas, John Mark, and others. "If we confess our sins, he is faithful and just to forgive us our sins, and to cleanse us from all unrighteousness" (I John 1:9). Full forgiveness and restoration are also part of God's wonderful provision for us in Christ Jesus. Don't let the devil cheat you out of that!

CHAPTER NINE

Demons: Superstition or Reality?

THE CHAPTER OUTLINED:

I. The Existence of Demons
1. Jesus Christ believed in the reality of demons
2. Not only did the Son of God cast out demons . . .
3. The whole New Testament teaches the existence of demons

II. The Origin of Demons
1. Demons as disembodied spirits of a pre-Adamic race . . .
2. Demons as the offspring of . . . angels and women
3. Demons as fallen angels

III. The Nature of Demons
1. Demons are spirits
2. Demons are evil by nature
3. Demons know of their ultimate doom

SUGGESTED BACKGROUND DEVOTIONAL READING

Monday—The Promise of Signs (Mark 16:15-20)

Tuesday—Devils Obey Christ (Mark 1:21-28)

Wednesday—The Tragedy of an Empty Life (Luke 11:21-26)

Thursday—Devils Believe and Tremble (James 2:14-20)

Friday—Who Hides Behind the Idol? (Ps. 106:34-38; I Cor. 10:20-21)

Saturday—The Unsparing God (II Peter 2:1-9; Rom. 8:32)

Sunday—Spurious Exorcists in Trouble (Acts 19:9-17)

In the last few years the newsstands and bookstores of North America and Europe have been flooded with books, magazine articles, and newspaper accounts of demon activity and its related subjects. Ever since the release of "The Exorcist" as a movie, the public has been buying anything that is written on the subject of demons; and the more sensational the story, the bigger its sale.

When some of my friends and acquaintances heard that I was working on a study of the world of unseen spirits, they began to send me a large number of newspaper clippings and periodicals, as well as books and booklets. All of this material was relative to the subject of demons. Some of the things that are written on the subject are worthless, an insult to the human mind. Some of the books are stimulating and interesting, and a few are very enlightening and helpful. For those who desire to do some research on the subject of demonology, I strongly recommend a book entitled *Biblical Demonology* by Merrill F. Unger (published by Scripture Press Publications). Dr. Unger has presented to the public a very valuable study of demonology, based upon the Word of God. Other books that have been especially helpful to me in preparing this study on demons are Hal Lindsey's *Satan Is Alive and Well* (published by Zondervan Publishing House), and *The Bible, the Supernatural, and the Jews,* written by McCandlish Phillips (published by The World Publishing Company). An exhaustive study on demon possession, entitled *War on the Saints* was published in England over 60 years ago. It was written by Mrs. Penn Lewis, in collaboration with Evan Roberts, and was printed by Alfred Tacy at the Excelsior Press, Leicester. There are 343 pages of small print which may try the reader's eyes and patience. However, to the person who is willing to really dig into things, the book will provide much food for thought and some surprise.

Within the limited space of this study, I want to present two brief chapters on the subject of Demonology. The first is devoted to the study of the existence, origin, and nature of demons. The second chapter is given to the consideration of the phenomena of demon possession.

The word "demon" is simply the Anglicized form of the Greek words *daimon* and *daimonion,* found frequently in the Greek New Testament. In the King James Version these words are usually rendered "a devil" or "devils." However, this word must not be confused with Satan who is the "diabolos" or "slanderer." As a rule, wherever the word "devil" appears in the Authorized Version without the definite article, it should read "demon." The same is true of the plural "devils," which should be understood as "demons." A careful reading of the four Gospels reveals that the terms "demons," "evil spirits," and "unclean spirits" are used interchangeably, all referring to the same kind of beings of the unseen world.

I. The Existence of Demons

When I was a little boy growing up in rural Germany, some of the men amused themselves with scaring the daylights out of children by telling ghost stories. I well remember how my heart would pound when I had to go out into the dark by myself. And if I heard any strange noise, shivers would run down my spine. Of course, I never let anybody know that I was ever scared, but pretended that I was very brave. In this I was a hypocrite.

Well, what about demons, do they really exist, or are they just a part of old superstitions? Are they the invention of men who wanted to scare the fearful? There are plenty of people who laugh at the mention of demons—who treat the subject as a joke. But demons are no joke, they are real. There doubtless are superstitions about them and ghost stories that are the product of human imagination. Those fakes do not affect the existence of real demons at all. I am no longer scared by ghost stories and superstitions have no place in my life. But I firmly believe in the reality of demons, of evil spirits who are abroad in the world, carrying on their evil work. How can I be so sure that demons are real? Here is why:

1. Jesus Christ believed in the reality of demons. This fact alone settles the question for me as it does for every true believer. If it can be ascertained beyond reasonable doubt that Christ believed in the reality of demons, and that He led others to believe likewise, then we are compelled to accept one of three conclusions. Either there are demons in the world as Christ said there were; or—Christ was mistaken (in which case He is not the Son of God from heaven and, therefore, not able to save us from sin); or—He deliberately deceived His followers about the matter (in which case He is not sinless, not to be trusted, and not fit to be our Saviour). Therefore, the real question for us to consider is whether Christ really did believe in the reality of demons. We cannot accept either the thought that He could be mistaken, or that He deliberately deceived His followers.

Christ repeatedly commanded demons to come out of persons who were possessed of them: "For he said unto him, Come out of the man, thou unclean spirit" (Mark 5:8).

"When Jesus saw that the people came running together, he rebuked the foul spirit, saying unto him, Thou dumb and deaf spirit, I charge thee, come out of him, and enter no more into him. And the spirit cried, and rent him sore, and came out of him . . ." (Mark 9:25-26).

"And Jesus rebuked him, saying, Hold thy peace, and come out of him. And when the devil [demon] had thrown him in the midst, he came out of him, and hurt him not" (Luke 4:35).

". . . And Jesus rebuked the unclean spirit, and healed the child, and delivered him again to his father" (Luke 9:42).

2. Not only did the Son of God cast out demons, but He gave His disciples authority to do so. "And when he had called unto him his twelve disciples, he gave them power [*exousia,* authority] against unclean spirits, to cast them out, and to heal all manner of sickness and all manner of disease" (Matt. 10:1).

"Heal the sick, cleanse the lepers, raise the dead, cast out devils" (Matt. 10:8; cf. Mark 16:17; Luke 10:17; Acts 5:16).

The overall evidence of the inspired record is so strong, so convincing, so natural and straightforward, that there is no room to question the fact that Jesus believed in the reality of demons. He talked with them and they talked to Him. He commanded and they obeyed Him. Some men argue that those demons who Jesus commanded to come out of people were in reality certain sicknesses or diseases. Dr. Merrill F. Unger in his book, *Biblical Demonology,* has answered that suggestion clearly when he asks: "What kind of disease was it that cried out, 'What have I to do with thee, Jesus, thou Son of the most high God?' (Mark 5:7). Since when has a monstrous physical distemper appeared which begs permission to enter into a great herd of swine and destroys them in a few fleeting moments? The substitution of 'spirit' (Luke 10:20) for 'demons' (v. 17) shows beyond all doubt that actual spiritual entities are meant, and not mere diseases."

3. The whole New Testament teaches the existence of demons. Aside from the Gospels, we find references to demon activities in a number of the books of the New Testament. The writer of Acts reports some interesting encounters with demons by some of the apostles and evangelists. In the earliest days of the infant Church they brought those "which were vexed with unclean spirits [to the apostles]: and they were healed every one" (Acts 5:16).

Philip, the deacon who became an evangelist, made use by faith of the

Lord's promise and; "unclean spirits, crying with loud voice, came out of many that were possessed with them" (Acts 8:7). Paul and his missionary companions were pestered for days by a woman who was "possessed with a spirit of divination." Finally, Paul "turned and said to the spirit, I command thee in the name of Jesus Christ to come out of her. And he came out the same hour" (Acts 16:18).

While in Ephesus, Paul preached the gospel of Christ and the Lord backed him up with miracles, including the expulsion of demons (cf. Acts 19:12). Then followed one of the most interesting episodes involving demons recorded in the Bible, when some spurious exorcists tried to cast out demons on their own. The results were most embarrassing to the exorcists (cf. Acts 19:13-16).

When writing to Timothy, Paul by inspiration declared that the Holy Spirit definitely revealed that in the latter days people would be led astray by "seducing spirits, and doctrines of devils [demons]" (I Tim. 4:1). James presents us with the inspired information that demons believe in God and tremble (cf. James 2:19).

So far in this study I have not mentioned the Old Testament. This omission is not because the Old Testament is silent on the subject of demons, but because the New Testament references are quite sufficient. One of the important revelations of the Old Testament is the fact that demons are both the promoters and real objects of idolatry. The reader is invited to carefully consider the following Scripture passages: Leviticus 17:7; Deuteronomy 32:17; II Chronicles 11:14-15; Psalm 106:35-37. Compare these verses with I Corinthians 10:20-21.

The conclusion of the matter is that the Bible certainly teaches the existence of demons. For all who believe that the Bible is the infallible revelation of God to man in its original form, the question of demon existence is therefore settled.

II. The Origin of Demons

There is some confusion among writers on the subject of demonology as to the origin of demons. Somewhat to my surprise I discovered that God in His Word does not clearly reveal their origin. Apparently, the Lord in His wisdom decided that we did not need to know the origin of demons. He was greatly concerned that we should know about their activities and evil design, and how to resist them. I also believe that although the Word of God does not give a clear statement on the origin of demons, there are nevertheless clues, signs, and inferences that do suggest an answer to the question of their origin. Writers on the subject present three main theories, namely:

1. Demons as disembodied spirits of a pre-Adamic race of humans. This theory is based upon the premise that the earth existed in a perfect state for an unknown length of time after its creation. And that it was covered with many forms of life, including a race of beings who were at least much like the present human race. The premise includes the belief that the whole world of life in that age was destroyed. This included the supposed pre-Adamic race of responsible beings, because they fell in with Satan and were judged with him. The judgment is supposed to have been the disembodiment of their spirits, thus having to spend eternity without a body in which to express themselves.

The biggest problem with this theory of the origin of demons is that the premise upon which it is based is an altogether unproven theory. It seems to me that in order to get a pre-Adamic race of intelligent and responsible beings out of the Bible, you will first have to write it in. Of course, I recognize the fact that when the Bible does not definitely state the origin of demons, that students with inquiring minds will search for possible answers. Nor do I find fault with such a search. We should be careful that we do not become dogmatic with our opinions when there is no proof from the Word of God to back them up.

2. Demons as the offspring of a union between angels and women. This view is based upon an interpretation of Genesis 6:2-4 which records that before the Flood "the sons of God saw the daughters of men that they were fair; and they took them wives of all which they chose. . . . There were giants in the earth in those days; and also after that, when the sons of God came in unto the daughters of men, and they bare children to them, the same became mighty men of old, men of renown." It is the opinion of many Bible scholars that these "sons of God" were angels who left their first estate (Jude 6) and cohabited with women, resulting in a race of wicked beings which were destroyed in the Flood. Other well-known Bible scholars hold that the "sons of God" were the godly descendents of the Seth line, while the "daughters of men" were ungodly descendents of the Cain line.

It is not within the scope of this study to enter into a long discussion as to which of the two interpretations is to be preferred. Again, it behooves us to avoid being dogmatic on an interpretation which cannot be verified elsewhere in the Word of God. One of the main arguments advanced in favor of the "angels with women" interpretation is the fact that the designation "the sons of God" is never used of human beings in the Old Testament, but always refers to angels. While this is true, the argument loses all its force when we discover that it never refers to fallen angels but to the heavenly host. I have not been able to find one instance where fallen angels are called "sons of God."

A few of the "angels with women" interpretators hold that demons are the disembodied spirits of the offspring of the unnatural union between angels and women. It is only fair to point out that many of the Bible scholars who hold that angels did cohabit with women, do not connect this with the origin of demons. Most seem to hold that these fallen angels who supposedly committed such a monstrous crime are the spirits who are reported to be kept in chains of darkness until the time of final judgment for them (cf. II Peter 2:4; Jude 6).

3. Demons as fallen angels. According to this view, demons are those angels who joined Satan's rebellion against God and who for the present time remain free in the universe to cooperate with Satan in his opposition to God.

While it is true that there is no clear statement in the Word of God that will settle the matter, it does appear that the identification of demons as fallen angels has a number of Biblical truths in its favor. For one thing, we know that Satan has a kingdom of spiritual beings. We also read that he has his own angels who seem to constitute that kingdom (cf. Matt. 25:41; Rev. 12:7). Demons obviously display many of the characteristics of Satan. Like Satan the "murderer," they torment humans whom they possess (cf. Mark 5:1-5). As does Satan the "liar," they operate by deceiving and are determined to lead people away from God and His Truth (cf. I Tim 4:1). When it comes to the peculiarity of demons always seeking to dwell within a human being, we are informed that Satan also "entered into" Judas (John 13:27). Apparently Satan will also take control of the Antichrist who is to come.

Demons are called "evil spirits" (Luke 7:21; Acts 19:12-16). The Greek word translated "evil" in these verses is *poneros,* meaning wicked, malignant. This description is highly significant because Satan is called *ho poneros,* "the wicked one" by our Lord (Matt. 13:19, 38), and by the Apostle John under the inspiration of the Holy Spirit (I John 2:13, 3:12, 5:18). Satan is evil personified, and demons are like him in their nature. It seems to me that most likely they are fallen angels who rebelled with Satan in the long ago.

III. The Nature of Demons

While the origin of demons is not definitely revealed, we need not be ignorant about what they are like, for they are well described in the Scriptures.

1. **Demons are spirits.** The designation "spirit" is applied to demons at least 41 times in the New Testament. "Spirit" is used in various ways in the Word of God. When speaking of living beings other than human, the word "spirit" is usually accompanied by a qualifying adjective, such as the "Holy Spirit," "ministering spirits," and "evil spirit." Generally speaking, "spirit" stands in opposition to the material. It refers to an intelligent being without an earthly body: "A spirit hath not flesh and bones, as ye see me have" (Luke 24:39). Demons then are intelligent and responsible beings of that great realm of unseen spirits. As spirits they are not subject to the laws of nature as we are, nor are they visible to the natural eye.

2. **Demons are evil by nature.** They are wicked, opposed to God, and antagonistic to man. The adjective used most frequently to describe their nature is "unclean," and is found ten times in the Gospel of Mark alone (Mark 5:2, 8, 13, and others). The Greek word translated "unclean" which is used to describe these spirits is *akathartos,* found 30 times in the New Testament. It is used almost exclusively of demons, 21 times as "unclean spirit" or "spirits" and twice translated "foul spirit" (Mark 9:25; Rev. 18:2). The *Analytical Greek Lexicon* defines the word as meaning impure, unclean, lewd, foul. Demons are unclean, dirty, foul, lewd—all the way through. Their malicious nature is seen in the fact that they always seem to inflict mental and physical torment upon the persons whom they control. Demons are out to corrupt and destroy people into whose lives they are permitted to have access. Anyone who in any way gives them an opportunity to gain some kind of control in his life is certainly inviting mental and spiritual, if not also physical disaster.

At this point I feel led to relate a personal experience. It happened in 1926 when I was 20 years old. We lived on a farm in northern Germany. I was the eldest son at home at the time and along with two younger brothers and several sisters managed my mother's farm. My mother's sister and husband, with their children, lived on a farm about six miles away.

Our two families visited together quite often, and as first cousins we knew each other well. The eldest daughter of my aunt was the same age as myself and I will call her "Anna," which was not her real name. Anna was very religious and conscientious. Both of us were members of the same Roman Catholic Church, and she took her religion seriously. One day we got word that Anna was ill. Apparently something had happened to her mind. It had come on her suddenly while she was weeding in the garden. She became restless, sullen, and unmanageable. The doctor prescribed rest, and when she did not improve, he suggested that a change of scenery might help. The family considered this and decided that our home would be the logical place for such a change. The girl knew us well, had been at our place quite often, and certainly would be treated with tender love. One day the father and Anna arrived via horses and wagon. All seemed well until a few hours after the father had gone home. Suddenly things began to happen. Anna seemed to be a completely different person. She cursed, swore, took God's name in vain, literally spit out curses at us, and used the most vile language any of us had ever heard. She also became violent, threw things at us, and we had to restrain her. A family council was quickly called and my mother suggested that I had better take her home. As soon as the horses were harnessed, we climbed into the wagon and the two of us headed for her home, sitting side by side.

After riding in silence for a while, I began to talk to her and she answered me. She seemed more like her former self. Then I turned to her and asked her why she had cursed so terribly. We had never known her to use an ugly word, and I was quite sure that she had never cursed before, or used vile and filthy language. When I asked what made her do it she visibly cringed, but closed her mouth and refused to answer my questions.

At home her condition worsened and the doctor advised that she be placed in a mental hospital. It was decided to take her to a Catholic institution in the city of Munster. Her father asked me to accompany them on the train, and we left her there with the nuns. About three months later official word was received by the father that Anna was healed, and he went to the city to bring her home. Anna was really healed and appeared to be her sweet former self again, except that she was somewhat somber and subdued.

After about a month or so Anna, with some of her family, came to visit us. It was a Sunday afternoon and the visit was an enjoyable one. Sometime during the visit Anna asked if she could talk to me in private. When we were alone she looked at me and said with tears in her eyes: "Bernt" (my nickname at home) "do you remember when you asked me why I had cursed and used such awful language?" When I answered that I remembered, she continued: "I was forced to say those things. There was a devil in me, and he made me say it. There was nothing that I could do about it. I did not want to talk like that and tried not to, but the devil in me forced me to do it."

I might add that "Anna" is still living. She has never had that kind of trouble again. I have told the experience exactly as it happened. My purpose in relating it is to show that demons are evil, wicked, unclean, and lewd. I believe that my cousin had temporarily come under the control of a demon. How this had come about, I do not know. Nor do I have any knowledge of how she was delivered. I do know that she later thought she had been controlled by a demon, and I am sure that she was set free. While she was subject to the control of another being, she was an altogether different person, and her language was foul and blasphemous in the extreme. At that time I was not born again, though outwardly religious. Now I read that when Satan shall take possession of the Antichrist, that man will blaspheme in language so vile and vicious that even the callous world will be astonished (cf. Rev. 13:4-6).

3. Demons know of their ultimate doom. "And, behold, they cried out, saying, What have we to do with thee, Jesus, thou Son of God? art thou come hither to torment us before the time?" (Matt. 8:29).

There is a *time* determined when both Satan and his angels will be in hell without hope of escape (cf. Matt. 25:41). They believe in God "and tremble" (James 2:19). Although they believe in God and know that their defeat and ultimate doom is certain, they do not repent or change their attitude. It is part of their very nature to be set against God and His plans, and to do all they can to oppose Him.

One fact of great interest to us is that *demons always obeyed Christ.* They always seemed to know Him, which demonstrates their super intelligence (cf. Mark 1:23-24; Matt. 8:29). Whenever and whatever Christ commanded them, they obeyed Him. Not only is this a testimony to the deity of the Son of God, but it also tells us where our safety lies from the power and influence of demons. When Christ and His love fills our hearts and we walk in fellowship with Him, demons cannot harm us. When their advances are resisted in the name of Jesus, they will leave us alone. It is the empty soul they seek to invade. Moral reform alone is not enough, Christ must fill the life. Jesus told it like this:

"When the unclean spirit is gone out of a man, he walketh through dry places, seeking rest; and finding none, he saith, I will return unto my house whence I came out. And when he cometh, he findeth it swept and garnished. Then goeth he and taketh to him seven other spirits more wicked than himself; and they enter in, and dwell there: and the last state of that man is worse than the first" (Luke 11:24-26).

CHAPTER TEN

Demon Possession

THE CHAPTER OUTLINED:

I. Important Facts about Demon Possession
1. Demon possession . . . confused with demon influence
2. Demon possession is not . . . "a familiar spirit"
3. Demons always seem to seek a home in a body . . .
4. Demon possession at the time of Christ's first coming

II. Manifestations of Demon Possession
1. Demon possession resulted in self-inflicted torture
2. Demon possession . . . mental and physical disorders
3. Demon possession was accompanied by recognizing Jesus
4. Demon possession was marked by . . . physical strength
5. Demon possession is indicated by a distinct "other" personality

III. Demon Possession and Exorcism
1. Christ . . . commanded the demons to leave their victims
2. Christ told His disciples to cast out demons

IV. Questions People Ask
1. Does demon possession occur today?
2. Can a saved person become possessed by a demon?

SUGGESTED BACKGROUND DEVOTIONAL READING

Monday—"Sitting at the Feet of Jesus" (Luke 8:26-35)

Tuesday—Witnessing Begins at Home (Luke 8:38-40)

Wednesday—Testing the Spirits (I John 4:1-6)

Thursday—Demons and Their Doctrines (I Tim. 4:1-8)

Friday—The Temple of the Holy Spirit (I Cor. 3:16-17; 6:18-20)

Saturday—Don't Give the Devil an Opening (Eph. 4:20-27)

Sunday—"Kept by the Power of God" (Phil. 4:4-7)

By demon possession we understand that an evil spirit has taken possession of a person and exercises control over that person's will, voice, and actions. When speaking of demon possession, the Greek New Testament uses the word *daimonizomenoi,* which literally means "demonized," that is, being under the control of a demon.

Does this sound like a myth out of medieval times, ridiculous in our day of scientific discoveries and research in human behavior? But, hold on a minute! I have watched as one person took control over another person's mind and will, and made him do things the victim had never thought of doing. They called that hypnotism and said that he was "hypnotized." We have all seen people who had temporarily lost control of themselves while under the influence of too much alcohol (sometimes called "spirits"). Some people are almost completely controlled by that evil monster and we call them alcoholics. There are thousands of our young people who are drug addicts. Their bodies and minds are enslaved to this habit-forming plague to the extent where they will steal, sell their bodies, and even kill to obtain the drug that controls them.

Seeing that human minds and bodies do come under the control of earthly minds and powers, is it incredible that man might come under the control of a superior being? A being that comes out of the unseen, but very real realm of spirits.

We are going to take a close look at what the Word of God has to say about demon possession. The Bible must be our guide in this study, else we will be caught in all sorts of speculations and stories which, while interesting, cannot always be checked out as to their reliability.

I. Important Facts about Demon Possession

1. Demon possession must not be confused with demon influence. Believers are warned about the influence that demons will exert, endeavoring to lead them astray from the truth of God's Word (cf. I John 4:1; I Tim. 4:1). The influence of evil spirits abounds on all sides, but both saved and unsaved may resist this influence. Once a person is possessed by a demon, he is subject to the will of that spirit and is helpless against it.

2. Demon possession is not the same as having "a familiar spirit" (Lev. 19:31; 20:27). Having "a familiar spirit" speaks of persons who voluntarily consult an evil spirit for information. Such a person is known as a medium. This phenomenon falls under the study of spiritism, which will be dealt with in another chapter. Demon possession has to do with persons who against their will are under the control of an evil spirit (although they may have been partly responsible for their condition). They are victims of an evil spirit, whereas the medium is a willing partner with the spirit. The difference can best be appreciated by noting that having "a familiar spirit" was declared in the Law given through Moses (Lev. 20:27) to be a spiritual crime, punishable by death. In contrast, those possessed by demons were treated by our Lord with tender compassion and delivered.

3. Demons always seem to seek a home in a body, whether human or animal. "And all the devils besought him, saying, Send us into the swine, that we may enter into them. And forthwith Jesus gave them leave. And the unclean spirits went out, and entered into the swine . . ." (Mark 5:12-13). "When the unclean spirit is gone out of a man, he walketh through dry places, seeking rest; and finding none, he saith, I will return unto my house whence I came out" (Luke 11:24).

Quite naturally we wonder why demons have an obsession to inhabit a body. There are at least two reasons that seem to be implied in the Bible. The first is the indication that dwelling in a body seems to give them "rest." To be without a body is like restless wandering in a dry desert. The Greek word *anapauo* ("rest") is translated "refresh" as often as "rest." To inhabit a body seems to provide some refreshment for the evil spirit. The second plausible reason for evil spirits seeking a body is that this gives them an instrument through which they can express themselves in the physical world. Through a human body the spirit has a speaking voice (cf. Mark 5:7-10), strength to act, to torment, and even to attack (cf. Acts 19:13-16). While outside the body, evil spirits can suggest evil to a person, but once the spirit takes possession within, he can make the person do evil.

Without trying to be facetious, I suggest that indwelling a human body makes existence a bit more interesting for the evil spirit who knows that his eternal doom is certain. Therefore evil spirits seek to possess human beings and express themselves through them before their time of eternal torment comes (cf. Matt. 8:29).

4. There was a great wave of demon possession at the time of Christ's first coming. The first three Gospels abound with reports of demon possession and the deliverance through Christ. This should be no surprise to us. It was the inevitable collision of light and darkness. One of the declared purposes of Christ's coming in the flesh was to "destroy the works of the devil" (I John 3:8). The first promise of the Saviour's coming included the declaration of "enmity" between the serpent and his seed, and the Seed of the woman (Gen. 3:15). When Christ finally appeared, Satan marshaled all his forces to oppose and hinder the Son of God. Demons could not attack Christ personally, but they centered their activities on the inhabitants of the region where He worked.

According to the New Testament, there will be another wave of extreme demon activity at the time of Christ's Second Coming. This also is to be expected, for at that time Christ will complete the defeat of Satan and shut him up for a thousand years. For a preview of the awesome activities of demons during that time the reader may turn to such Scripture passages as Revelation 9:1-11; 12:7-9; 16:13-14.

II. Manifestations of Demon Possession

This presents an intriguing and yet baffling study. The manifestations of demon possession reported in the New Testament are quite varied, as are also the persons who were possessed. The first three Gospels report cases of both men and women being possessed. One boy who was brought to Jesus was possessed of a demon from his childhood (cf. Mark 9:17-27). One girl was delivered from a demon (cf. Mark 7:25-30). Most were possessed by a single demon. One victim had "many devils" (evil spirits) as we see in Luke 8:30. Mary Magdalene was delivered of seven demons (cf. Mark 16:9; Luke 8:2). There is also the fearful story of what the evil spirits forced their victims into doing.

1. Demon possession resulted in self-inflicted torture. Taking a close look at the man with the many demons, we behold a dreadful situation. According to Mark's account in chapter 5, verses 1-15, this man lived in a graveyard, "crying" (screaming), and "cutting himself with stones." Luke adds that the man wore no clothes, and that he "was driven of the devil [demon] into the wilderness" (Luke 8:27-30). Matthew tells us that the man was "exceeding fierce, so that no man might pass by that way" (Matt. 8:28). All three writers report that when the spirits entered the swine, the whole herd of "about two thousand" became violent and committed self-destruction.

In the case of the possessed boy the physical torment is even more appalling. Mark's Gospel presents this vivid description: "And one of the multitude answered and said, Master, I have brought unto thee my son, which hath a dumb spirit; And wheresoever he taketh him, he teareth him:

and he foameth, and gnasheth with his teeth, and pineth away. . . And when he saw him, straightway the spirit tare him; and he fell on the ground, and wallowed foaming. And he asked his father, How long is it ago since this came unto him? And he said, Of a child. And ofttimes it hath cast him into the fire, and into the waters, to destroy him . . ." (Mark 9:17-22). When Jesus ordered the spirit to come out of the lad, "the spirit cried, and rent him sore, and came out of him: and he was as one dead . . ." (Mark 9:25-26).

The boy's father was evidently convinced that the evil spirit was trying to destroy the lad through suicide. A number of times the New Testament writers report that persons possessed of demons were "vexed" by the evil spirits (cf. Matt. 15:22; Luke 6:18; Acts 5:16). Demons are evidently much like their leader, Satan, who delights in hurting and destroying human life.

2. Demon possession was accompanied by mental and physical disorders. The man dwelling in tombs was evidently insane as a result of the many demons tormenting him. Luke reports that when the people came from town to see what had happened, they "found the man, out of whom the devils were departed, sitting at the feet of Jesus, clothed, and in his right mind" (Luke 8:35). This suggests that he had been out of his right mind before. The father of the possessed boy stated that his son was a "lunatic" (Matt. 17:15).

In a number of reported demon possessions the victims were subject to physical disorders and diseases. One victim was both blind and dumb. When Jesus delivered him from the demon, the man was also healed of his physical disorders. His sight was restored as well as his ability to speak (cf. Matt. 12:22). Other similar cases are found in Matthew 9:32; Mark 9:17, 25; Luke 11:14; 13:11, 16.

The fact that lunacy, blindness, dumbness, and deafness often accompanied demon possession has led some critics to say that the possessions were nothing more than insanity, epilepsy, blindness, and other diseases and deformities. This explanation may sound reasonable to the unwary, but it cannot be maintained in the light of the overwhelming evidence to the contrary. Jesus dealt with diseases as diseases, and with demons as living beings who sometimes afflicted their victims with disease. Those demons spake, cried out, knew Christ, they raged, asked permission to enter swine, talked about the time and place of their coming torment, and so forth. If we can trust the Bible at all, then those spirits whom Jesus commanded to come out of people, were living spirits, and not blindness or insanity, deafness or epilepsy. Most diseases that Jesus healed were the results of natural causes, but some of them were inflicted by demons.

3. Demon possession was accompanied by a recognition of Jesus. The persons who were possessed of demons always seemed to know Jesus. They even knew who He *really* was, the Son of God from heaven. There is no plausible explanation of this except the one given by the writers of God's Word who report that it was the evil spirit speaking through the voice of the one possessed (cf. Mark 1:23; 5:6-7; Luke 4:41; Acts 19:15).

4. Demon possession was marked by extraordinary physical strength. The man possessed with the many demons continued to break all fetters and chains with which he was bound (cf. Luke 8:27-29). The demon-possessed man at Ephesus attacked seven young men, tore their clothes off them, and sent them running—"naked and wounded" (Acts 19:15-16).

5. Demon possession is indicated by a distinct "other" personality. When we compare all the Biblical accounts of demon possession we find that when a demon asserted himself, the victim displayed a distinct "other" personality. This expressed itself in actions, strength, language, and intelligence altogether foreign to the normal personality. This "other" personality is one of the evidences of demon possession and distinguishes the medium from those who are actually possessed by an evil spirit. The medium retains his or her own personality. Writers who describe cases of modern demon possession often report a complete change in moral behavior in the "other" personality. This was certainly true in the case of my cousin which I described in the preceding chapter.

III. Demon Possession and Exorcism

The word "exorcist" comes from the Greek word *exorkistes* which was the title given to persons who claimed to drive out an evil spirit by the use of certain rituals. That such a practice existed in ancient times is seen in the story of what happened to certain "exorcists" in Ephesus as related by Luke in Acts 19:13-16. This is the only place in the Bible where the word *exorkiston* appears. It is never used of the work of Christ in delivering people from demons. The casting out of demons reported in the Bible reveals the following facts:

1. Christ, by His own power and authority, commanded the demons to

leave their victims. "And Jesus rebuked him, saying, Hold thy peace, and come out of him. . . . For with authority commandeth he even the unclean spirits, and they obey him" (Mark 1:25, 27; cf. Luke 8:29). Jesus would openly "rebuke" the demon, tell him to "hold thy peace" (literally, be gagged), and command him to come out. In every instance the Lord was obeyed instantly. This we would expect when the Son of God spoke.

2. Christ told His disciples to cast out demons. This casting out was to be done in the Lord's name and by His authority. "Then he called his twelve disciples together, and gave them power and authority over all devils, and to cure diseases" (Luke 9:1). "And the seventy returned again with joy, saying, Lord, even the devils are subject unto us *through thy name*" (Luke 10:17, cf. v. 1). In the Great Commission to His disciples Jesus promised that He would back them up as they would preach the Gospel, with certain "signs," and one of those signs would be: "*In my name* shall they [believers] cast out devils" (Mark 16:17).

The records indicate that in the early years of the Church the casting out of demons was done in the name of Christ. "But Paul, being grieved, turned and said to the spirit, I command thee in the name of Jesus Christ to come out of her" (Acts 16:18).

From the study of all cases mentioned in the New Testament involving the casting out of demons we may safely conclude that only true believers in Christ are authorized to cast them out, and this can be done successfully only in the name of Christ. This one case reported where the unsaved tried to cast out a demon in the name of Christ, was met with the worst kind of failure (cf. Acts 19:13-16).

IV. Questions People Ask

1. Does demon possession occur today? Yes, there are cases of demon possession in our time. Writers on Biblical Demonology, who represent the conservative viewpoint in their interpretation, are almost unanimous in answering the question in the positive. Until recent times it has seemed that as the light of the Gospel spread in the world, cases of demon possession decreased. This kind of development is not difficult to understand. In the first place, Satan and his angels thrive in spiritual darkness. They cannot work as well where the light of the Word of God abounds. Furthermore, idolatry has all but ceased where the Gospel of Christ has come to stay. Dr. Merrill Unger in his book *Biblical Demonology* comments: "But there are demons now, the claims of the critics notwithstanding. They are present today working in multitudinous less overt, but none the less real ways. Not only are there demons in so-called Christian lands, but where Christianity and civilization have not penetrated deeply, demon possession and the grosser demonic manifestations are present too. The modern mission field furnishes abundant evidence of this fact to the honest inquirer after truth. The reason is quite obvious. There the Gospel coming into head-on collision with entrenched Satanic opposition and the pagan darkness of centuries, brings the operation and power of evil supernaturalism into sharper focus, and reveals demonic activity amazingly similar to that which occurred in the days of our Lord's ministry."

In recent years there has been a growing rejection of the Gospel in civilized lands. Along with this there has come a great upsurge of interest in spirits and related subjects. Such topics include extrasensory perception, witchcraft, astrology, Satan worship, fortune telling, and all sorts of occultism. There is a growing interest in the ancient religions of the East, along with plain idolatry involving blood sacrifices. The search is on for new experiences in the world of the unknown through "trips" in drugs. All of this is an open invitation to the evil spirits for a comeback in demon influence and demon possession in the Western World. Anyone who starts experimenting with fortune telling, black magic, witchcraft, or "acid trips," is inviting trouble with evil spirits.

While serving as pastor of a church in Ohio, several years ago, I was called upon to deal with what I firmly believe was a case of demon possession. The victim was a young man who had married a girl of excellent Christian background, and it was she who brought her husband to me. My associate in the pastorate was an older man, a real brother in the Lord by the name of James Cook. The two of us met with this young man in the sanctuary of the church, where we encouraged him to tell his story. He began by telling us that several years before he had become interested in what he called "black magic." He had become acquainted with a man who practiced black magic and who could perform unbelievable tasks. Our young friend had ended up taking part in a ritual in which he had "sold himself to the devil."

All of this had happened in Texas. Since the day of the ritual, he had experienced trouble with a spirit which forced him to curse and to blaspheme. When he married, the spirit became more bold, driving him until he could no longer hold a job or live a normal life. He told us that before he could wash his face in the morning, the spirit demanded that he repeat certain blasphemies 20 times. If he refused to comply, his hands and arms would not function. The same thing would be repeated with other aspects of getting dressed. As a result he could no longer get to work on time, had lost one job after another, and the family was destitute. He wanted to be free of the evil spirit, but expressed doubts about this possibility because he had agreed to serve the devil.

It took this man several hours to tell his frightful story. He was obviously under great pressure and perspired profusely. We had a short recess in which we talked to the man's wife to check on his story. Pastor Cook was convinced that we were dealing with a real demon. Both of us were quite apprehensive and had a short prayer meeting. After consulting together on what to do next, we called the young man back to the sanctuary and spent some time explaining God's plan of salvation to him. We then placed our hands upon his head and I called on the evil spirit to come out of the man in the name of Jesus Christ, the Son of God.

My faith must not have been very strong because I was surprised at the results. There was an immediate change in the man. His eyes lost that haunted look. He seemed greatly relieved and was jubilant at being delivered. There were tears of joy shed by his wife. He no longer had trouble getting dressed, and in a few days he had found a job and was working regularly. He soon made a public confession of Christ as his Saviour and was baptized. There was a definite change, and he was present at every service.

It would be great to stop at this point of the story, but it would not be right. After about three or four months of faithfulness to the Lord, the man began to drift a little. He began to be absent—first at the midweek prayer service and soon at some of the Sunday services. I talked with him about his need of Christian fellowship, pointing out that he could not afford to tempt the Lord with carelessness after all that God had done for him. There were promises and excuses, but the trend toward indifference continued. He began to avoid me. His attitude seemed to say that he now could make it without the Lord. Within a few more months he was back in trouble. He could not get dressed, lost his job, and obviously was back under the control of an evil power.

Was this man's conversion real or pretended? I do not know. I am only telling what happened as far as could be seen. The evidence of demon possession was convincing. The sudden change seemed to us miraculous.

The whole episode was a sobering experience, and I want to sound a solemn warning against the danger of experimenting with anything that is even remotely connected with evil spirits.

2. Can a saved person become possessed by a demon? It has been argued that since the believer's body is indwelled by the Holy Spirit of God (cf. I Cor. 6:19), it cannot at the same time be inhabited by an evil spirit. This sounds reasonable. However, there are some questions that come to mind. What about the two natures of the believer, may not an evil spirit work through the old nature? Is it not true that the Holy Spirit will fill only what is yielded to Him? Does not Satan have access to the believer to tempt him and even to take him "captive by him at his will" (II Tim. 2:26)?

As far as I can determine, there is no case recorded in the New Testament of demon possession involving a Christian believer. However, there are warnings against the power and activities of both Satan and his evil spirits, which indicate that a believer can be influenced by them. Paul's warning concerning "seducing spirits" (I Tim. 4:1) implies that those who "depart from the faith, giving heed" to those spirits, are believers, for how can they "depart" from what they did not have?

There is a real possibility that Christians may be led astray by demon influences. This danger is acute when believers respond to curiosity concerning spirit forces and experiment with them in any way. Demon influence may lead people astray into false doctrines when they accept visions and dreams as a basis for belief and action, or when they listen to false teachers. There is danger of being led astray when a person seeks an emotional experience at any cost, for a demon may provide that experience. Demons will take advantage of spiritual inactivity, such as neglect of the Word of God and private prayer. Wherever any ground is yielded to the adversary, there evil spirits will try to get a foothold. The inspired admonition of the Apostle Paul is most appropriate when he warns: "Neither give place to the devil" (Eph. 4:27). The meaning of this is that believers are not to give the devil an opening. The following quotation from Dr. Merrill Unger's book *Biblical Demonology* sums up the matter:

"Demonic influence may assume a great variety of forms. Its sign is always departure from the faith, or the body of revealed truth, and may manifest itself in open apostasy (I Tim. 4:1), or in doctrinal corruption or perversion of the truth, evident in a multiplicity of cults and sects, producing Christian disunity (I John 4:1-2). If an orthodox creed is adhered to, it may show itself in ritualistic formalism, or empty adherence to the letter without the spirit (II Tim. 3:5), or in hypocrisy (I Tim. 4:2-3). Demon influence in doctrine leads to corrupt conduct and practice (I Cor. 10:16-22), resulting in worldliness (II Tim. 3:4) and uncleanness (II Peter 2:10-12)."

One thing we may be sure of, and that is the fact that when Christ fills our lives and the Holy Spirit is in control, when God's Word is studied and received, then neither Satan nor his evil spirits can enter or even influence us. Satan with his whole kingdom of evil spirits cannot defeat the power of the Living Word and the written Word of God.

While concluding this study there comes to my mind the old and well-worn story of the company superintendent who was interviewing candidates for the job of driving a stagecoach in the mountains of the West. He asked each candidate how close he could drive to the edge of a precipice and still feel safe. As one candidate after another assured him that he could drive within a foot or less of the edge without fear, he was dismissed. When one candidate answered the question by saying that he did not know how close he could come to the edge without being scared, but that he was surely going to stay away from it as far as possible—he immediately got the job.

How close to the edge of spirit contact can a Christian come and still be safe? The safest thing to do is to stay as far away as possible, rejoicing in the salvation of the Lord, and giving Satan no opening at all.

CHAPTER ELEVEN

Divination, Spiritism: Can the Dead Communicate With the Living?

THE CHAPTER OUTLINED:

I. Artificial Divination and the Word of God
1. The meaning of astrology
2. Astrology and the Word of God

II. Spiritism, the Employment of Demons
1. Genuine Spiritism calls for a medium . . .
2. Spiritism and supposed contact with the dead
3. The case of Saul and the medium at Endor

SUGGESTED BACKGROUND DEVOTIONAL READING

Monday—Why Pray When You Can Worry? (Dan. 2:13-23)

Tuesday—God Knows the Answer (Dan. 2:19-28)

Wednesday—The Folly of the Horoscope (Isa. 47:12-15)

Thursday—Where to Find Out about the Future (II Peter 1:16-21)

Friday—Books That Are No Longer Needed (Acts 19:17-20)

Saturday—Fully Furnished (II Tim. 3:13-17)

Sunday—Too Late to Send a Message (Luke 16:23-31)

"There shall not be found among you any one that maketh his son or his daughter to pass through the fire, or that useth divination, or an observer of times, or an enchanter, or a witch, or a charmer, or a consulter with familiar spirits, or a wizard, or a necromancer. For all that do these things are an abomination unto the Lord: and because of these abominations the Lord thy God doth drive them out from before thee" (Deut. 18:10-12).

"Divination" is a general term descriptive of the various practices for the obtaining of secret information by methods which are contrary to the will and holy character of God. This general term includes a long list of ancient and modern arts such as astrology, palmistry, cardlaying, sorcery, spiritism, necromancy, and a host of other more or less mysterious means and methods for the discovery of the unknown, from Ouija boards to crystal balls, and seances.

There is a tremendous revival of divination and such practices in the world today, especially among the young. Considering the fact that we live in the age of science and technology, this is an astounding phenomenon. Surprisingly, nothing new has been added, it has all been done before. The people who lived 4,000 years ago had divination down to a fine art and practiced it as a religion. In ancient Babylon the diviners attained the highest honors in human society. They formed a brain trust for the emperors (Dan. 2:2), and in general became so important and indispensable to society that no political decision could be made, no military mission undertaken, no new house built, not even a journey begun, until the diviners had been consulted and had pronounced the appropriate time for its successful end.

As was the case with Nebuchadnezzar's brain trust of astrologers, sorcerers and soothsayers who could not know what the king had dreamed and were exposed as impostors, so much of today's divining is based on fraud, involving the use of tricks, ventriloquism, sleight of hand, and so forth. However, there is also the possibility of Satan and his spirit-helpers using any of the various practices of divining to work their evil designs upon human beings. All of these practices are strongly condemned in the Word of God and are not to be used by God's people. The reasons for this will be presented later in this chapter.

The different practices of divination are usually divided into two groups, sometimes called "artificial" and "inspirational" divination. In artificial divination the secret information is supposedly obtained through the correct interpretation of certain combinations of nature or chance. These include such phenomenon as the lines in the palms of the hand, the relative position of the moon, sun and stars on certain days and their influence (supposed) on human affairs; the chance falling of the cards, the flight of birds; the information of the clouds, gazing into a crystal ball; or even the placement of the tea leaves at the bottom of the cup.

So-called inspirational divination has to do with the supposed or real contact of a person with a spirit who supplies the information asked for by a client. The professional who has contact with such a spirit is generally known as a medium. In the Bible such a person is said to have "a familiar spirit," or a "spirit of divination."

I. Artificial Divination and the Word of God

In the Lord's injunction against seeking guidance by the use of divination (cf. Deut. 18:9-14), a number of practices are named. Divination was practiced by reading objects of chance, like the dregs left in a cup. The "witch was really a sorcerer who used charms, brews, potions, with which he promised to influence the future of the client. The "enchanter" used secret formulas of his own. Since the objective of this study guide concerns itself with spirits, I am presenting only one example of the use of objects in divination. That is the practice of astrology, which was widely used in ancient times and has become very popular today.

1. The meaning of astrology. *Webster's New World Dictionary* defines astrology as "A pseudo science claiming to foretell the future by studying the supposed influence of the relative positions of the moon, sun, and stars on human affairs." The word "pseudo" means false, pretended, counterfeit, not corresponding to reality.

Though it is a pseudo science, astrology has been around a very long time. It is followed by millions of people today. Horoscopes (the charts based upon the zodiacal signs and the position of the planets) appear in most of the daily newspapers of this country. According to the Research Institute of Public Opinion at Lake Constance, 63 percent of the German people have been occupied with astrology. Hitler, it is said, had five full-time astrologers advising him. The case of Rudolph Hess, who landed in England during World War II for the purpose of persuading the British to cast in their lot with Germany against Russia, is one of the most remarkable demonstrations of the influence of astrology on the leaders of the

Third Reich. According to Kurt Koch in *Between Christ and Satan,* the horoscope of Rudolph Hess had predicted that he was destined by fate to bring about a reconciliation with England.

The daily horoscope contains mostly platitudes and vague admonitions such as "Keep busy," "Don't worry about what can't be helped; carry on in a constructive way," and so on. It is difficult to think that intelligent people will believe that the position of the heavenly bodies has anything to do with the lives of human beings. However, the evidence says that millions are greatly influenced by these charts. Many persons almost live by the horoscope. In such cases it can greatly disturb a person's mind, cause fears and depression—especially with people of sensitive minds. A serious following of the daily horoscope can also impair a person's initiative and result in a warped personality.

2. **Astrology and the Word of God.** Perhaps nowhere else is astrology as well described and its claims exposed as being false, as in God's Word. The Lord addressed the Babylonian people and their rulers through Isaiah, saying: "Stand now with thine enchantments, and with the multitude of thy sorceries, wherein thou hast labored from thy youth; if so be thou shalt be able to profit, if so be thou mayest prevail. Thou art wearied in the multitude of thy counsels. Let now the astrologers, the stargazers, the monthly prognosticators, stand up, and save thee from these things that shall come upon thee. Behold, they shall be as stubble; the fire shall burn them . . ." (Isa. 47:12-14).

The "astrologers" were those who viewed the heavens, or "divided the heavens." In today's language, they were the professionals who cast a horoscope. The "stargazers" were of the same family, who looked up into the heavens and contemplated the message of the heavenly bodies. The "monthly prognosticators" were those who got their information from the moon, at the time of each new moon, therefore "monthly."

God's Word is replete with condemnations of all efforts to secure superhuman information by any other means than that of God himself. God's will is plain enough. For His own people all such seeking is sin. This covers every kind of fortune telling, by whatever method—cards, tea leaves, palmistry, or the position of the stars. Those who have renounced the world and have received Christ as Saviour and Lord of their lives must not insult the Lord by consulting the instruments of Satan. The infallible Word of God is all that the child of God needs to guide him and inform him on what is to come (cf. II Peter 1:19-21). We read that when the people of

Ephesus turned to Christ, "many of them also which used curious arts [magic arts] brought their books together, and burned them before all men: and they counted the price of them, and found it fifty thousand pieces of silver. So mightily grew the word of God and prevailed" (Acts 19:19-20). Those people had found Christ and no longer had any use for the books and charts that originated from satanic influences.

The Word of God presents some definite reasons explaining why God's people must have nothing to do with the whole practice of fortune telling and divining, such as:

(a) *"There is no light in them"* (Isa. 8:19-20). The whole range of fortune telling and divining has no beneficial information to offer to man.

Of great significance is the fact that all the highly regarded brain trust of Babylon, including the "magicians, and the astrologers, and the sorcerers, and the Chaldeans" (Dan. 2:2) had no way of knowing what Nebuchadnezzar had dreamed (v. 10). But God revealed it, along with the significance of the dream, to Daniel and his friends in answer to prayer (vv. 27-28). At a later date, the same branches of diviners, including the "soothsayers" were stymied by another dream of the king (Dan. 4:6-7). And again Daniel, who was in touch with God, had the answer (vv. 8, 19-27). When years later the fingers of a man's hand appeared and wrote, "MENE MENE, TEKEL, UPHARSIN" on the wall of the banquet hall, Nebuchadnezzar's grandson Belshazzar "cried aloud to bring in the astrologers, the Chaldeans, and the soothsayers" (Dan. 5:7). This whole new crowd of diviners failed to help the trembling king. They could not even read the writing, let alone interpret its meaning. Finally, old and by then forgotten, Daniel was remembered; and he had the correct answer (Dan. 5:13, 25-31).

In the light of what the Word of God has to say, I believe that the whole business of divination has no trustworthy information to offer. I do not mean to say that none of their predictions come to pass. But they also err, and there is no one−human being, Satan, demon, or angel−who foreknows the future apart from what God reveals. "There is no knowledge in them."

(b) *Divination has its background in idolatry.* "When thou art come into the land which the Lord thy God giveth thee, thou shalt not learn to do *after the abominations of those nations"* (Deut. 18:9). These words form the preface to the condemnation of a list of actions which were practiced by the idolatrous nations around them. At the head of that list is the ban on human sacrifices which were offered to the idol Molech. Astrology particularly had its origin in the worship of the heavenly bodies. Israel soon followed the example of those nations and offered sacrifices "unto Baal, to the sun, and to the moon, and to the planets, and to all the hosts of heaven" (II Kings 23:5). The Hebrew word *mazzaloth* which is translated "planets" in the King James Version is rendered "twelve signs" in the Revised Version margin. The Oxford Annotated Bible translates the word "constellation." The reference is undoubtedly to the twelve signs of the zodiac as suggested in the Amplified Old Testament.

(c) *The practice of any kind of divination is an "abomination" to God.* "For all that do these things are an abomination unto the Lord" (Deut. 18:12). Those who seek information from superhuman sources insult and disgust the God of heaven. He wants His children to trust Him with their problems and requests and to look to Him for guidance. For this purpose He has given us His infallible Word. All employment of mystical sources are open to satanic influence, are damaging to human souls, and are therefore hateful to God. The Bible declares that the use of divination *"defiles"* a person (Lev. 19:31).

II. Spiritism, the Employment of Demons

Spiritism, which is also called Spiritualism, is defined in *Webster's New World Dictionary* as "the belief that the dead survive as spirits which can communicate with the living, especially with the help of a third party, called a medium."

Raphael Gasson, a former medium states in *The Challenging Counterfeit:* "It is well to constantly remember that Spiritualism is an attempt to communicate with what are presumed to be the spirits of the dead. Those who indulge in this cult give themselves up to demons, who pose as 'spirit guides' and 'loved ones' and Spiritualists become ready to give obedience to what are actually demons whether they realize it or not."

The Word of God has a great deal to say about Spiritism and vigorously condemns its practice in any form. The following outline will acquaint the reader with the major facts, gathered from a study of all the Biblical references on the subject.

1. Genuine Spiritism calls for a medium who has contact with a demon. Such a medium is said to have a "familiar spirit." "And the soul that turneth after such as have familiar spirits . . ." (Lev. 20:6). "A man also or a woman that hath a familiar spirit" (Lev. 20:27; cf. Lev. 19:31; I Sam. 28:3-9; Isa. 8:19; 19:3; 29:4). King Manasseh is said to have "dealt with familiar spirits" (II Kings 21:6).

A "familiar spirit" is an evil spirit or demon, and is called "familiar" because the medium is considered to be on intimate terms with such a spirit. In modern Spiritism these demons are known as "spirit guides," and each medium is supposed to have such a guide.

2. Spiritism and supposed contact with the dead. Seeking contact with the spirits of the dead seems to have been the major use of "familiar spirits" by mediums in Old Testament times (and such is also the case with modern Spiritism today). The medium claimed to be able to call up the spirit of the dead person, asked for by the client, through the services of the "familiar spirit" or spirit guide. Technically this calling on the spirits of the dead is known as necromancy. The Hebrew for the "necromancer" in Deuteronomy 18:11 when literally translated means "one who inquires of the dead."

This brings up the question: Can the dead communicate with the living? Nothing has stirred public interest in this question more in recent times than the case of the late James A. Pike, bishop of the Episcopal Church. Bishop Pike (who denied a number of the fundamental doctrines of the Christian faith) was led to believe that he had received communications from his son James Jr., who had taken his own life on February 4, 1966. Drawn by a series of peculiar happenings, the bishop consulted a medium who supposedly got him in contact with his son. A Mrs. Maren Bergrud who served as secretary to the bishop accompanied him. She also took her own life after having been a witness to a number of seances. Bishop Pike published the results of the seances in a book which caused quite a stir.

In the spiritualistic sessions which the bishop attended, the medium would go into a trance. And a voice similar to that of the bishop's son, and alleging to be his son, would speak through the lips of the medium. Some of the seances were taped. Among other things, the voice told the bishop that (in that other world) he had seen nothing to make him "any more inclined to believe in God." When questioned whether he had seen Jesus, the voice asserted that they talked of Him only as an "example" not a "Saviour." The voice denied the personality of God, defining Him as "the Central Force." Bishop Pike himself was found dead in the barren desert near the Dead Sea on September 7, 1969.

What does the Word of God say about the question of communication from the dead? In the first place the whole experience of Bishop Pike is contrary to the Word of God. The message of the Bible is that God is a personal God who is very much interested in each human soul, and who sent His Son to redeem man from the bondage of sin. The alleged voice of the deceased James Pike Jr., said that God was "the Central Force." Christ declared that He came from the Father who had sent Him that "the world through him might be saved" (John 3:17). The supposed voice of the dead insisted that the spirits of the dead talked of Christ only as an example and not as a Saviour. Whom are we to believe? There is terrible deceit here. We remember that false doctrines are said to be planted by "seducing spirits," and that such teachings are the "doctrines of demons" (I Tim. 4:1). We are warned by the Word of God not to believe every spirit, but to "try the spirits," and that "every spirit that confesseth not that Jesus Christ is come in the flesh is not of God" (I John 4:1-3).

Bishop Pike ignored the emphatic teaching of God's Word that man is not to seek contact with the dead through a medium. "Regard not them that have familiar spirits" (Lev. 19:31). "And the soul that turneth after such as have familiar spirits . . . I will even set my face against that soul, and will cut him off from among his people" (Lev. 20:6). "There shall not be found among you . . . a charmer, or a consulter with familiar spirits, or a wizard, or a necromancer" (Deut. 18:10-11).

Many proofs or signs were given through the different mediums that it was actually the voice of James Pike Jr., who was speaking. These signs include the citing of certain habits peculiar to the young man, and the mentioning of certain events out of his past which the mediums had no way of knowing. The answer to this is that the familiar spirit or spirit guide of the medium spoke through the voice of the medium, *while impersonating the dead.* The dead do not come back. They cannot come back except by the power of God and He has prohibited it. Evil spirits are deceptive by nature. They know about us and can produce faked evidence to deceive a person into believing that a departed loved one is speaking. They can even imitate a voice.

To sum up the case of Bishop Pike's supposed communication with his deceased son, I quote Dr. Merrill Unger who wrote in *The Haunting of Bishop Pike:* "On the basis of God's Word, the personalities contacted in a seance are not departed human beings, but rather fallen angels in the service of Satan. These spirits impersonate the dead to lure the living into a land where Christ is 'Just another person' and time repairs all the evil of the past. . . . Demonic forces won the first round with the bishop when he departed from Biblical faith, opening his mind to the teaching of demons." To this I would like to add that the bishop lost the second round when he ignored God's warning and consulted a medium.

3. The case of Saul and the medium at Endor (I Sam. 28:3-19). This is a unique experience, the only one like it in the whole Bible. The Lord had withdrawn from Saul because of the continued disobedience of the king. Facing a serious battle with the Philistines and getting no response from God, Saul went to a woman with a familiar spirit to seek contact with Samuel who had died some time before. The king disguised himself, for he had carried on a vigorous campaign against mediums in times past; and, if recognized, would not be able to persuade any medium to help him (cf. I Sam. 28:3, 8-9).

When the medium (she is never called a witch in the Bible) asked whom from among the dead Saul wanted to talk with, he asked for Samuel (v. 11). As the woman was about to do her thing, something happened that struck terror to her heart, for Samuel actually appeared.

It is apparent that this was a special act of God for the purpose of bringing Saul into judgment. It was not the medium who brought up Samuel, for she was astonished, to put it mildly (v. 12). This was not the usual procedure. It was not what the woman expected. It had never happened like that before, and the woman was shocked and scared. As a result the woman abandoned her role as a medium and a direct conversation resulted between Saul and Samuel, without the voice of the medium.

Another remarkable difference between that incidence and the usual seances of mediums is the fact that Samuel's words were direct, clear, and in complete harmony with God's attitude toward sin and righteousness. Whereas the usual alleged contacts with the dead produce only vague and mysterious information; and when touching on doctrinal matters, they declare things completely out of harmony with the holy character of God (cf. Rom. 1:18).

CONCLUSION

God alone can bring back the dead, and I believe that He did so in the case of Samuel. God alone deserves our worship and our spiritual contact in prayer and fellowship. God's Holy Spirit leads us to see that Satan is forever trying to find an entrance in a human life. If he gets a foot inside the door, he starts his work of creating disorder and ruin.

We are living in a time of great spiritual hunger. The souls of men and women are empty, a world condition similar to that which existed at the time of the first coming of Christ. Satan is taking advantage of this emptiness by leading them into his cults which are counterfeits of the reality of God's way of salvation. Should not our hearts be stirred with compassion and resolve that by the grace of God we will tell people of the Son of God who is "the way, the truth, and the life," and who promised to give us water to drink that satisfies forever? Satan knows that he has but a short time left to do his evil work. Do we know that we have but a short time left in which to reach men and women for Christ?

CHAPTER TWELVE

The Human Spirit: A Brief Study of Man— Body, Soul and Spirit

THE CHAPTER OUTLINED:

I. **The Origin of Man**
  1. Man had his origin in the direct creative act of God
  2. The entire human race descended from the same original parents

II. **The Image and Likeness of God in Man**
  1. God is spirit, and man is a spiritual being . . .
  2. God's image in man is seen . . . in his ability to reason
  3. There is a likeness to God in man's moral consciousness
  4. God's image in man is seen in man's free will

III. **Man Divided into Body, Soul and Spirit**

IV. **Facts about the Human Spirit**
  1. The word "spirit" is used in the Bible in many ways
  2. Because of sin, man's spirit is separated from God
  3. The question arises as to the origin of man's spirit

SUGGESTED BACKGROUND DEVOTIONAL READING

Monday—"Fearfully and Wonderfully Made" (Ps. 139:1-14)

Tuesday—In the Image of God (Gen. 1:26-31)

Wednesday—"Worship . . . in Spirit and in Truth" (John 4:21-26)

Thursday—"The Natural Man" (I Cor. 2:9-16)

Friday—"We Shall Be Like Him" (I John 2:28—3:3)

Saturday—The Sanctity of the Human Body (I Cor. 6:12-20)

Sunday—When Our Knowledge Will Be Unlimited (I Cor. 13:1-13)

"I will praise thee; for I am fearfully and wonderfully made . . ." (Ps. 139:14).

The Psalmist had been meditating on the greatness of God and His interest in man. As usually happens when man's mind is occupied with God's greatness and grace, a wave of joy and wonder filled the Psalmist's heart and he exclaimed: "I will praise thee; for I am fearfully and wonderfully made." The wonders of a human being are many and most of them surpass the limits of our comprehension.

Consider the wonders of the human body, with over 300 different movements and functions, known as bars, ball bearings, beams, buffers, cables, pulleys, joints, pumps, pipes, sockets! Man has a computer brain that defies description. His ears are sophisticated receiving sets. The eye is the finest camera ever invented—self-loading, self-cleaning, self-winding, self-focusing, and instant self-developing—taking millions of pictures each day. The human stomach is a laboratory with automatic ignition and combustion systems. And words fail us when we speak of the heart, or the great network of nerves, our intricate voice box, or the marvelous thermostat that keeps the temperature the same on the inside no matter what it may be on the outside. Praise the Lord! "For I am fearfully and wonderfully made."

There is also the wonder of man's mind. "Thou madest him to have dominion over the works of thy hands; thou hast put all things under his feet" (Ps. 8:6). Even though much impaired and retarded by sin, man's mental capacity is still a source of wonder. By much searching he found a way to harness the power of electricity into a light bulb and picture tube and discovered a way to go to the moon and return. Or think of the accomplishments in the field of music, with its great hymns and symphonies! And what of the masterpieces in the realm of literature and art?

Consider the wonder of man's conscience, that little umpire within, which calls every play, whether it be fair or foul! And then consider the possibilities of each human being for God and good, or Satan and evil, with capability to be a Paul or a Judas, a Martin Luther or an Adolph Hitler, to be the temple of the Living God, or the instrument of the devil! Yes, man is fearfully and wonderfully made.

The Biblical study of man is a subject of vast dimensions, and leads us into mysteries that are beyond the range of our present understanding. This can easily be seen by reflecting on the first mention of man in the Bible, a passage which is the seedbed of all that is revealed about him:

"And God said, Let us make man in our image, after our likeness: and let him have dominion over the fish of the sea, and over the fowl of the air, and over the cattle, and over all the earth, and over every creeping thing that creepeth upon the earth. So God created man in his own image, in the image of God created he him; male and female created he them" (Gen. 1:26-27).

The implications of these statements introduce us to the great mystery of man and foreshadow the magnitude of the task of trying to explain him. Who can comprehend the possibilities involved in being made in the image and likeness of God? It should be clearly understood therefore that this present study of man is little more than a framework of what God's Word has to say on the subject of man.

I. The Origin of Man

1. Man had his origin in the direct creative act of God. "So *God created man* in his own image, in the image of God *created* he him; male and female *created* he them" (Gen. 1:27). This revelation was fully endorsed by the Lord Jesus Christ according to Matthew 19:4. Many attempts have been made to accommodate the record of the Bible to the theory of Evolution. This is impossible to do without violating the very principle of the inspiration of the Sacred Scriptures. The Word of God declares that man was created by God. This was not done over a period of millions of years, but all at once; not by evolving him from the bottom, but by starting him at the top, in the image and likeness of himself. The Word tells us that man became a living soul when God breathed into the formed body "the breath of life" (Gen. 2:7). That inbreathing resulted in an immediate, perfect man. To reconcile that with the theory of Evolution is an impossible task.

2. The entire human race descended from the same original parents. There are no two species of human beings. This is Biblical and has the full support of science. The Word of God declares: "And Adam called his wife's name Eve; because she was *the mother of all living*" (Gen. 3:20). "And [God] hath made *of one blood* all nations of men for to dwell on all the face of the earth" (Acts 17:26). The facts of life support this. Human beings of any race on earth can intermarry with persons of any other race or tribe, and instead of resulting in sterility, this usually produces increased fertility. I am not an authority on Evolution, but I do believe the

Word of God, and it says that God created man in God's own image. I have
not seen anything yet that gives me reason to doubt the Word of God.

II. The Image and Likeness of God in Man

The image and likeness of God in which man was created (Gen.
1:26-27) may not refer to the physical body of man. At least there is no
evidence for such likeness in the Word of God. God is spirit and as spirit
He is invisible to the natural eye. Aside from physical appearance, and in
spite of the awful blow which God's likeness in man received in man's Fall,
some evidences of that likeness are still apparent.

1. **God is spirit, and man is a spiritual being, with a human spirit.** Jesus
said: "God is a Spirit: and they that worship him must worship him *in
spirit* and in truth" (John 4:24). The inspired apostle wrote: "The Spirit
itself beareth witness with *our spirit,* that we are the children of God"
(Rom. 8:16; cf. Luke 8:55). In his human spirit man can have fellowship
with God. Of all earth's creatures, this is true only of man. Real prayer and
true worship is when man in his spirit is occupied with God.

2. **God's image in man is seen in man's intelligence, in his ability to
reason.** "Come now, and let us reason together, saith the Lord . . ." (Isa.
1:18). Man is invited to come and let God reason with him. God does
reason with man. This I know from experience, and I lost the argument.
There is therefore a kinship of minds, a relationship of reasoning power. In
pointing this out I am not forgetting that our reasoning power is less than
a drop in the ocean in comparison with the wisdom and knowledge of
God. This is what Paul must have had in mind when he wrote: "For now
we see through a glass, darkly; but then face to face: now I know in part;
but then shall I know even as also I am known" (I Cor. 13:12). Our
understanding now is limited, but the kinship of minds is there, and in the
day when we shall be transformed to be like Jesus, our understanding also
will be perfect.

God apparently delights in creating. He is the creator of the universe,
and what a universe! What a mind God must have! But man also delights in
making things. He has a craving for making and perfecting almost anything. He feels the wind and makes a windmill. He watches the bird in its
flight and cannot rest until he finds a way to fly. Man beholds the moon
and dreams about getting there. Man is born with a craving to know.

3. **There is a likeness to God in man's moral consciousness.** "Which

shew the work of the law written in their hearts, their conscience also bearing witness, and their thoughts the mean while accusing or else excusing one another" (Rom. 2:15). God is absolutely holy. Man knows what is right and what is wrong. He has a moral consciousness which God has placed within man in the beginning. And though man's conscience is greatly dulled by the Fall, and though man tries to find all kinds of ways to get around it, it is still present within. And so man is without excuse. Think of Pilate wrestling with his conscience! Watch him washing his hands trying to quiet that conscience and show the Jews that he was not responsible for sending Jesus to His death!

4. God's image in man is seen in man's free will. God is free and sovereign in His will (Eph. 1:11). Man also is a free moral agent with the freedom of choice on almost every level, especially on the moral level. Even God won't interfere with that sacred right of man to choose, for He gave man that right. Almost the last verse in the Bible (before its final benediction) emphasizes man's free will in that wonderful invitation: "And the Spirit and the bride say, Come. And let him that heareth say, Come. And let him that is athirst come. And *whosoever will*, let him take of the water of life freely" (Rev. 22:17).

III. Man Divided into Body, Soul and Spirit

The Bible presents man as a tripartite being. All three parts of man are found in the account of Adam's creation. "And the Lord God formed man of the dust of the ground [his body], and breathed into his nostrils the breath of life [the spirit], and man became a living soul" (Gen. 2:7). In the New Testament all three parts of man are mentioned together, but in a different order as follows: "And I pray God your whole spirit and soul and body be preserved blameless unto the coming of our Lord Jesus Christ" (I Thess. 5:23).

There is a great deal of misunderstanding about man's soul, as to what it is and what its relationship is to man's spirit. It is not my purpose to burden the reader with a great deal of technical phrases or controversial opinions. It is true that the word translated soul in the Old Testament is also used of the life of animals. It is also true that the terms of soul and spirit are sometimes used interchangeably. Nevertheless there is a difference between them. The reason why both terms seem to be speaking of the same thing is that these two, the spirit and the soul of man, are never separated from each other. This cannot be said of the body and the soul, or the body and the spirit.

For the sake of clarity and simplicity, let us think of man like this: You *have* a body. The apostle calls this your "earthly house" (II Cor. 5:1). In the Genesis account we are told that this body is made up of earthly elements (Gen. 2:7). When death comes, *you* leave this earthly house, move out of it (II Cor. 5:6, 8). All right, so far so good. You *have* a body.

You also *have* a spirit. This is what God breathed into Adam. All human beings have a human spirit. "For what man knoweth the things of a man, save *the spirit of man* which is in him? Even so the things of God knoweth no man, but the Spirit of God" (I Cor. 2:11). Two different spirits are mentioned in this verse, the spirit of man which is the human spirit, and the Spirit of God which is the Holy Spirit. The same thing is true of Romans 8:16, which speaks of the Holy Spirit's witness with the human spirit: "The Spirit itself beareth witness with our spirit that we are the children of God." Paul speaks of "my spirit" (Rom. 1:9), "your spirit" (Gal. 6:18; II Tim. 4:22).

So you *have* a body, and you *have* a spirit at this very moment while you are reading these lines. Now comes the difficult part, for very likely you are ready to say that you also have a soul. But when you say it that way you are doing away with the difference between the soul and the spirit of man. You do not have a soul, unless you mean your spirit when you say soul. You *have* a body, and you *have* a spirit, but you *are* a soul. I am not a body. If I say that I am a body I will be talking of only one part of me. I am not a spirit, though I have a spirit. But I am a living soul. Look carefully at that seventh verse of Genesis, chapter 2. You will find here that God prepared a body for man and then added a spirit which came directly from Him, and thus man "*became* a living soul." This is what man is essentially, a living soul. "The first man Adam was made a living soul" (I Cor. 15:45).

The soul is you, the real you that lives now in your body. You are an individual person or soul, different from all other souls. If you think of your soul as your individual personality, you will not be far wrong from its use in the Bible. The complete *you* has a spirit with an eternal existence. You also have a body which dies and disintegrates when you leave it. Actually it is your spirit that leaves the body, but since that is all that you have after death, it is still you, the soul that leaves. If you are born again in your spirit, God will give you a new body in the resurrection, a glorified body, and then you will really be a wonderful person. You will find that angels are called spirits, but never souls. They are spirits but have no body. Man alone has a body and a spirit.

Some Bible teachers hold that the soul and the spirit are the same, but the Word of God makes a distinction between the two. The writer of Hebrews said that God's Word is "sharper than any two-edged sword, piercing even to the dividing asunder of the soul and spirit" (Heb. 4:12, cf. I Thess. 5:23).

Different expressions have been used by Bible teachers endeavoring to help us understand the meaning of body, soul and spirit. McCandlish Phillips points out that the body is the seat of man's world-consciousness, that the soul is the seat of self-consciousness, while the spirit is the seat of God-consciousness.

An animal has life and is conscious of living. This consciousness has a body and the whole is spoken of in the original Old Testament text as a soul. But the animal has no spirit. The self or soul of the animal, having only a perishable body, ceases to exist when death comes. But man has a spirit that exists forever and after death man continues in the spirit.

The Word of God repeatedly speaks of the soul as being in that other world beyond death. David, speaking of the resurrection of Christ a thousand years before Jesus was born into this world, wrote: "Thou wilt not leave my soul in hell [sheol] ; neither wilt thou suffer thine Holy One to see corruption" (Ps. 16:10). The Holy Spirit has given us an inspired interpretation of the meaning of this prohecy, which is found in Acts 2:25-31. While Christ's body was in the grave for three days, He himself went to Sheol (Hades in the Greek New Testament), that is, His spirit went there, and yet He is called soul. This means that He himself went to Hades, in His spirit. On the third day His spirit returned to His body which was now glorified. Then the Lord could assure the terrified disciples: "Behold my hands and my feet, that *it is I myself:* handle me, and see; for a spirit hath not flesh and bones, as ye see me have" (Luke 24:39). A spirit does not have flesh and bones, but the soul, the "I myself" of the risen Christ did have flesh and bones, for the soul with the spirit had returned to the body.

The reader is invited to consider two separate statements in Revelation which are instructive at this point. John, being permitted to enter the spirit world to witness a preview of events surrounding the return of Christ, reports: "And when he had opened the fifth seal, I saw under the altar the *souls* of them that were slain for the word of God, and for the testimony which they held" (Rev. 6:9). A little later John tells of seeing these same souls, now reunited with their glorified bodies, reigning with Christ on earth for a thousand years (cf. Rev. 20:4-6).

The spirit and soul of man are never separated. This fact causes some of the confusion about them in people's minds. At the moment of death, the spirit is separated from the body (cf. James 2:26), and the living soul, the conscious self is then only in the spirit, but very real and conscious.

IV. Facts about the Human Spirit

1. **The word "spirit" is used in the Bible in many ways.** It often stands for the disposition or attitude of a person or persons, such as "the spirit of slumber" (Rom. 11:8), "the spirit of meekness" (Gal. 6:1), and so forth. Don't let this bother you, for I heard a man say the other day: "I did not make it that time, but I am not giving up." Whereupon someone else said: "That is the spirit!" Of course, he meant "attitude." The Bible was written in a language and words which people then living understood. When the word spirit is used of the third Person of the Godhead, it is usually capitalized in our translations. Then there are evil spirits, and angels are called spirits. The word spirit is even used of the true meaning and intent of God's Word, called the "spirit" as opposed to the "letter" or outward form (cf. II Cor. 3:6).

2. **Because of sin, man's spirit is separated from God.** The Holy Scriptures indicate that in the unsaved person the spirit is dead toward God. Not dead in the sense of extinction (something death never means when used of man, in the Bible), but unresponsive to God, not able to function as the spirit was meant to function. The unsaved person is called "the natural man" (I Cor. 2:14). The Greek actually says that he is a "soulical" man. He is a living soul within a body, but his spirit is dead toward God—is not functioning. In this natural state man does not "receive" (does not welcome) the things of the Spirit of God, cannot even "know" them (understand them), because they are "spiritually discerned." When a person is born again by the "renewing of the Holy Ghost" (Titus 3:5), he receives a new life which is spiritual life, or eternal life, and he is now alive in his spirit. He can now worship God in spirit and in truth and have spiritual fellowship with the God of heaven and earth. There is now a tremendous change in the person, in the soul, which will express itself in

the disposition, the attitudes, and interests of the soul. In turn these will be expressed in the deeds of the body which is controlled by the soul.

The unregenerated man is "soulish" or *self-centered.* This is the great tragedy caused by man's Fall. When born again, the new life of God enters the spirit of man. The Holy Spirit comes to dwell in him, and that person is now *God-centered,* as he was meant to be. From thereon he chooses as to which center will predominate, the old self or the new center through which the Holy Spirit operates.

3. The question arises as to the origin of man's spirit. Does God create a new human spirit each time a baby is born? There are those who hold to this assumption, and this view is called "Creationism" in theological circles. The implications of the Word of God point to something else.

The Scripture indicates that when God created the first man, he placed within that man the power to reproduce his own kind: body, soul and spirit—the whole person. This is called Traducianism. Without entering into a lengthy discussion of this question, it does seem to me that this is the only logical conclusion to be drawn from the Word of God. When our first parents sinned, they received a sinful nature, a bend toward doing the wrong and not the right thing. This bend is quite overpowering, and is present, born into each newborn human being. If God created a new spirit for each new child, then He would be creating a fallen spirit, which is completely out of character with the God of the Bible. I am persuaded that when God created Adam and Eve, He made full provision for the reproduction of children who would be like them, with all the possibilities of the billions of different souls and personalities that were to come.

CONCLUSION

The course of this world is influenced by Satan whose aim is to keep man away from God. This is clearly demonstrated in the emphasis that is placed upon the physical and mental side of man, and the almost total neglect of the spirit of man. Great advances are being made in the study and understanding of the human body. This is a good thing and beneficial to us all. Tremendous strides have been made in recent days toward the understanding of the great mystery of the human soul, the self-consciousness of man, where fears and complexes arise. But where is the progress in the study of the spirit of man? Man's spirit gets hardly a line in the news and scarcely an hour of attention in the great learning processes of the world's educational institutions. I believe that one of the greatest mistakes of modern psychiatry is the ignoring of man's spirit while probing into man's mind and soul.

Christian reader, God has redeemed you and brought you into His own family. He has saved your soul from sin, and He desires that you should glorify Him "in your body, and in your spirit" (I Cor. 6:20). You are made in the image of God. And in the Person of God's Son your potential is the greatest wonder of all, for "whom he did foreknow, he also did predestinate to be conformed to the image of his Son, that he might be the firstborn among many brethren" (Rom. 8:29). Remember to praise Him, for you "are fearfully and wonderfully made."

CHAPTER THIRTEEN

What About Life After Death?

THE CHAPTER OUTLINED:

I. What Is Death?
1. Death is the penalty for man's disobedience to God
2. The primary meaning of death in the Bible is separation

II. What Happens When a Saved Person Dies?
1. At the moment of death, the believer will be with Christ
2. The believer will be conscious after death

III. Striking Illustrations of the Believer's Death
1. The believer's death is like going on a journey
2. The believer's death is . . . moving to a new home
3. Death to the believer is "gain"

IV. What Happens When the Unsaved Dies?

SUGGESTED BACKGROUND DEVOTIONAL READING

Monday—Are You Dead or Alive? (Eph. 2:1-10)

Tuesday—Where Did Death Come From? (Rom. 5:12-21)

Wednesday—Moving to our New Home (II Cor. 5:1-9)

Thursday—"Which Is Far Better" (Phil. 1:15-26)

Friday—"Ready To Be Offered" (II Tim. 4:1-8)

Saturday—Hell, and Who Goes There (Rev. 20:11-15)

Sunday—God Could Do No More (John 3:14-21)

An old English captain was relating to an admiring audience some of his experiences as a soldier in England's far-flung battle line. He told of his marvelous escapes and of the many wonderful things he had seen on sea and land under every sky. Every so often he would remark: "But I shall see more wonderful things than these." The listeners kept wondering what he meant because he was old and retired from the service. At last he cleared up the mystery when he ended his stories by saying: "But one day I shall see more wonderful things than these, in the first five minutes after death."

This last chapter will be a brief tour into that land beyond death. Our guide will be the infallible Word of God of which Jesus said that *it shall all be fulfilled.* There really is no other guide who can tell us anything about that land, for no man or woman living on earth knows a single thing about life after death except that which is revealed in the Word of God. Aside from what God has revealed about it, the greatest philosopher, the best scientist, and the most eloquent preacher knows no more about life after death than does the most ignorant man in town. Therefore we dare not speculate or wander off on our own, but must stick close to our guide.

I. What Is Death?

In order to learn all we can of life after death, we do well to acquaint ourselves with the Biblical view of death itself. What does the Word of God say about death?

1. Death is the penalty for man's disobedience to God. "But of the tree of the knowledge of good and evil, thou shalt not eat of it: for in the day that thou eatest thereof thou shalt surely die" (Gen. 2:17). "Wherefore, as by one man sin entered into the world, and death by sin; and so death passed upon all men, for that all have sinned" (Rom. 5:12).

2. The primary meaning of death in the Bible is separation. When the Word of God speaks of the death of a human being, it never means the end of existence, but the loss of function due to separation. It is somewhat like your automobile. If someone removed the battery from your car, the whole car would be dead. It would still exist, but it would not function. When man is said to be dead, he still exists according to the Bible. He just is not functioning properly. This is a most important principle to remember when considering the meaning of death.

There are three kinds of death mentioned in the Bible. They are:

(a) *Spiritual death,* which is man's separation from God caused by sin, and resulting in the cessation of the proper functioning of the spirit of man. God is holy and righteous and cannot have anything to do with sin except to judge and condemn it. With sin upon him, man is said to be "dead in trespasses and sins" (Eph. 2:1, 5; cf. Col. 2:13). Since this separation affects the whole man in every part, the person is said to be dead. This is the natural state of every man and woman who is outside of Christ. That this being dead in trespasses and sins is not the end is crystal clear. This is being dead while alive (cf. I Tim. 5:6), and this kind of death explains the otherwise puzzling statement of Christ to the man who wanted to wait to serve the Lord until after he had buried his father: "Let the dead bury their dead . . ." (Luke 9:60). The only remedy for spiritual death is the New Birth which is a spiritual birth.

(b) *Physical death,* which is the separation of man's spirit from the body, resulting in the body losing its function. "For as the body without the spirit is dead, so faith without works is dead also" (James 2:26). "And when Jesus had cried with a loud voice, he said, Father, into thy hands I commend my spirit: and having said thus, he gave up the ghost" (Luke 23:46). At the moment of physical death, man's spirit leaves the body. Paul calls this being "absent from the body" (II Cor. 5:8). This separation also affects the whole person and so the person is said to be dead, not his body only. The remedy for physical death is the resurrection.

Both spiritual and physical death were included in God's warning to Adam concerning disobedience. The Hebrew actually says: "In the day thou eatest thereof, dying thou shalt die" (Gen. 2:17). The moment he sinned, Adam died spiritually. He was separated from God, his spirit ceased to function toward God, and he was afraid. His physical death, though certain, did not take place until many years later.

(c) *The second death,* which is mentioned twice in the last book of the Bible (cf. Rev. 20:14, 21:8) and refers to the final judgment of the unsaved. This occurs at the end of the millennium when they will be resurrected and condemned to an eternal separation from God in the lake of fire. There the whole person will be completely lost to the very purpose for which God created man. The purpose being to glorify God and enjoy Him forever. For this death there is no remedy.

II. What Happens When a Saved Person Dies?

When a born-again person is overtaken by physical death, that soul or conscious self in his spirit leaves his body and enters a conscious existence in the intermediate state. The intermediate state is a term which stands for the state of existence during the time between a person's physical death and the moment of his resurrection at the Second Coming of Christ. Because the conscious self has left the body, that body is without life and immediately begins its dissolution. "The body without the spirit is dead" (James 2:26). "For we know that if our earthly house of this tabernacle were dissolved . . ." (II Cor. 5:1).

1. **At the moment of death, the believer will be with Christ.** This precious truth is made exceedingly clear in many passages of Scripture. "Therefore we are always confident, knowing that, whilst we are *at home in the body,* we are absent from the Lord: (For we walk by faith, and not by sight:) We are confident, I say, and willing rather to be *absent from the body,* and to be *present with the Lord*" (II Cor. 5:6-8). The word in the original Greek, translated "at home" in verse 6, and referring to our present life in the body, is exactly the same as the one translated "present" in verse 8. The Greek word is *edemeo* and means to live, to dwell, to make your home. So this passage of Scripture really says that even as now we are at home in our bodies, when once we have left this home, we will be at home with our Lord.

When speaking of his desire to depart this life while willing to stay around a while if that was God's will, Paul said: "For I am in a strait betwixt two, having a desire to depart, and to be *with Christ:* which is far better" (Phil. 1:23). If words have meaning, then this says that when the spirit of a saved person leaves the body at the time of death, he enters into the presence of Christ, which state is far better than our present one.

Jesus assured the repentant thief on the cross with the solemn promise: "Verily I say unto thee, Today shalt thou be with me in paradise" (Luke 23:43). The first Christian martyr died with the prayer: "Lord Jesus, receive my spirit" (Acts 7:59). All of this adds up to the blessed assurance that at the moment of death the believer in his spirit enters the presence of Christ.

2. **The believer will be conscious after death.** There are those who insist that the soul will be "sleeping" and not know anything after death. This view can only be arrived at by a very strained interpretation of the use of "sleep" in the Bible. The soul's consciousness is plainly taught and strongly implied in the Word of God.

The apostle John was permitted to view events in heaven which are recorded in Revelation. There he "saw under the altar the souls of them that were slain for the word of God and for the testimony which they held: and they cried with a loud voice, saying . . ." (Rev. 6:9-10). These souls are the martyrs of the first half of the Great Tribulation. We are particularly interested in their condition before their resurrection, and we note that they are conscious, that they cry out, and they are reasoning with God about something.

Paul, who had daily fellowship with his Lord by faith, spoke of life after death as being "far better" (Phil. 1:23), and as being "gain" (v. 21). How could it be "far better" if he would be unconscious, not knowing anything? The picture Jesus gave us in the 16th chapter of Luke of conditions after death can only be interpreted as a state of consciousness and continued interest in what is going on. While the lost man was "in torment," Lazarus was "comforted." That means consciousness.

III. Striking Illustrations of the Believer's Death

A wonderful change in man's attitude toward death came about when Christ finished His work of redemption through His sacrificial death and glorious resurrection. The reason for this change is best stated by the writer of the Book of Hebrews: "Forasmuch then as the children are partakers of flesh and blood, he also himself likewise took part of the same; that through death he might destroy him that had the power of death, that is, the devil; and deliver them who through fear of death were all their lifetime subject to bondage" (Heb. 2:14-15).

There had been a fear of death even among godly people who lived before the coming of Christ. All they could look forward to at death was to go to Sheol, a place where the spirits of the dead were. Unfortunately, the translators who prepared the King James Version really mixed people up when they rendered the word Sheol as "hell" 31 times, "grave" 31 times, and 3 times as "pit." The Greek word for Sheol is Hades, is found 11 times in the New Testament and is translated "hell" each time. This confusion and mistranslation has given birth to a number of false doctrines.

A brief explanation of Sheol and Hades (they are the same thing) is in order at this point. The words speak of a waiting place where the spirits of the dead were confined. There were two sections. One of them was for the unsaved which was known as "lowest sheol" (Ps. 86:13; Deut. 32:22). The reader will take notice that the King James Version calls it "hell." Jesus told us there was a "great gulf fixed" between the two sections. He called the place where the saved were by the suggestive term of "Abraham's bosom," where there was rest and comfort; while on the other side of the gulf, torment and misery held sway (cf. Luke 16:19-26). When Christ addressed the penitent thief, He promised they would meet that day "in paradise" (Luke 23:43).

Because Sheol was all the Old Testament saints could hope for at the time of death, there was a fear of death that held universal sway. They did not have the prospect of going to heaven when they died, even though there were some remarkable revelations of a future resurrection. Their salvation was still based on a promise. They were saved on credit and had to wait until that credit was made good. All this was changed when Jesus came. When He shouted "It is finished" (John 19:30), that credit was made good. God's promise had become an accomplished fact, and now the waiting spirits could be accepted in heaven.

During the time between Christ's death and resurrection, His spirit went to Sheol (cf. Ps. 16:9-10; Acts 2:24-31). The Holy Spirit revealed through Peter that while Christ (in spirit) was in Sheol, He made an announcement or proclamation: "For Christ also hath once suffered for sins, the just for the unjust, that he might bring us to God, being put to death in the flesh, but quickened by the Spirit: By which also *he went and preached unto the spirits in prison*" (I Peter 3:18-19).

We do not know the words of that announcement, but we can imagine that its theme was the same as His last announcement to the world before His death, which was the shout: "It is finished." God's promise of redemption was fulfilled. Satan was defeated and doomed. To the unsaved this was an announcement of certain and eternal doom. To the waiting souls of the righteous ones that was a message of greatest joy, for now they could join God's family in heaven.

When Christ arose and ascended to the right hand of the Father, He did not go alone. God's Word says that when He ascended on high, "he led captivity captive" (Eph. 4:8). The New English Bible translates this phrase: "He ascended into the heights with captives in his train." This seems to be a strong indication that when Christ returned to the Father after having completed His work of redemption, He took with Him all those souls of the Old Testament believers who had been confined to Sheol. They had been waiting for this day of deliverance. The announcement that the risen Christ has "the keys of hell [Hades] and of death" (Rev. 1:18) gives strong support to this belief. After God's salvation was completed, we find believers going directly to be with Jesus at the time of death. And the fear of death is gone for those who have put their trust in Him.

The New Testament presents a number of striking word pictures of the experience of going to be with Christ by way of physical death. These illustrations and experiences shed some light on what death will be like for believers when it comes.

1. **The believer's death is like going on a journey.** "Having a desire to depart, and be with Christ; which is far better" (Phil. 1:23). The Greek word translated "to depart" is *analusis* which is a nautical term and is found only twice in the Greek New Testament. Paul used the same idea in noun form a bit later when he wrote to Timothy about his impending death as a martyr: "For I am now ready to be offered, and the time of my *departure* is at hand" (II Tim. 4:6). *Analusis* was a word sailors used and literally means "to loose up anchor." Death for the believer is to pull up anchor in order to sail into another port. He enters that safe harbor which is the presence of our Lord, and which is "far better." Forgive the suggestion, but could it mean that while the anchor here is lifted and loved ones watch and finally turn and say: "He is gone," or "She is gone," that others on the other side are watching, too, and are saying: "He is coming," or "She is coming"?

2. **The believer's death is described as a moving to a new home.** In that wonderful series of word pictures that Paul gave us in II Corinthians 5:1-8, he speaks of the believer being absent from Christ while at home here in the body. But Paul was looking forward to the time when he would move out of this home and be "at home" with his Lord. As pointed out earlier in this chapter, the words "at home" in verse 6 and "present" in verse 8 are translations of the same word in Greek, which is *edemeo,* which means to be at home, to live there. Death for the Christian is moving from the earthly home into a new home with Christ.

3. **Death to the believer is "gain."** "For to me to live is Christ, and to die is gain" (Phil. 1:21). The Greek word is *kerdos* and Paul used it only twice, both times in the letter to the Philippians. The true meaning may best be seen by his use of it in chapter 3 and verse 7. Here he sums up the loss of his earthly standing as a Jew, for the privileges of the Gospel of Jesus Christ and all that he had found in Him, and he calls it a real "gain."

Even so is death a real gain, pure profit, for the person whose trust has been in Christ.

IV. What Happens When the Unsaved Dies?

The person who dies without Christ has nothing to look forward to but judgment and eternal separation from God. This is not a popular statement today, but it is certainly a Biblical fact. While the death and resurrection of Christ liberated the saved from Sheol, there was no change in the intermediate state of the unsaved. No truth is more plainly stated in God's Word than the fact that all who pass out of this life without Christ, who have rejected or neglected God's gift of salvation, offered and provided through His Son, will be lost eternally. At the time of death they enter Sheol where they will be confined until the final judgment. Of that judgment we read: "And whosoever was not found written in the book of life was cast into the lake of fire" (Rev. 20:15).

During His earthly ministry, the Son of God directed most of His teaching efforts toward the awakening of people to their desperate need of salvation from sin. One of His dramatic efforts was His description of the eternal state of the unsaved. Jesus called it the "fire that never shall be quenched: where their worm dieth not, and the fire is not quenched." This statement He repeated three times (Mark 9:43-48). Of this eternal state in the lake of fire, Sheol is but the anteroom, and it will become part of that lake of fire at the time of the final judgment (cf. Rev. 20:14). Others may try to take the fire out of the words of Jesus, but I cannot.

CONCLUSION

Jesus said: "For God sent not his Son into the world to condemn the world; but that the world through him might be saved. He that believeth on him is not condemned: but he that believeth not is condemned already, because he hath not believed in the name of the only begotten Son of God" (John 3:17-18).

Dear reader, I trust that you have responded to the gracious invitation of God to receive Christ as your Saviour and Lord. If there is any doubt about it, why not turn to Him now and ask Him to be your Saviour! He has promised that He will not turn you down. With Christ as our Saviour, life has real meaning and purpose, and at the end, a wonderful home. Without Christ man is lost, without an anchor for his soul and without hope or home in the end.

Imagine a cold and stormy evening in February: The wind is blowing strong and cold. A mixture of snow and rain is falling. It is bad to be caught out on such a night. Two men are walking down the road. The first is a wanderer. His collar is turned up and his head is bent low into the wind as he struggles against the elements. His face is passive. He is a wanderer without a home. He has no real goal, except to keep going, without anything to look forward to. He is enduring the elements.

Many people are like that spiritually. They have no spiritual goal or home. They are enduring what comes and have no hope except to keep going as long as possible. There is no looking forward to a home.

The second man, too, has his collar turned up against the elements. The same storm is blowing around him. But he is whistling a song, and there is a spring to his step and joy in his face. He sees a light up ahead, and that is where he is headed. It is his home where loved ones are waiting up for him. Comfort and fellowship are waiting there for him, and that makes all the difference in the world. His being out in the elements has meaning.

The person with Christ in his life is like the second traveler. He, too, faces the elements and storms, but there is meaning to life for him—for he is headed home.

Bibliography

Barnhouse, Donald Grey. *God's Freedom, Romans,* Vol. VI. Grand Rapids: Eerdman's Publishing Co., 1961.

Basham, Don. *Deliver Us from Evil.* Washington Depot, Connecticut: Chosen Books, Distributed by Revell, 1972.

Bavinck, Herman. "Death." *International Standard Bible Encyclopaedia,* Vol. II. Grand Rapids: Eerdmans, 1939.

Bounds, Edward M. *Satan, His Personality and Overthrow.* Grand Rapids: Baker Book House, 1973.

Cambron, Mark G. *Bible Doctrines.* Grand Rapids: Zondervan, 1954.

Chafer, Lewis Sperry. *Satan.* Findlay, Ohio: Dunham Publishing Company, 1919.

_____. *Systematic Theology,* Vol. II and Vol. III. Dallas: Dallas Seminary Press, 1947.

Chambers, Oswald. *Biblical Psychology.* London: Simpkin Marshall, 1941.

Davis, John J. *Contemporary Counterfeits.* Winona Lake, Indiana: BMH Books, 1973.

Davis, T. Witton. "Divination." *International Standard Bible Encyclopaedia,* Vol. II. Grand Rapids: Eerdmans, 1939.

Denham, J. F. "Demon." *The Popular and Critical Bible Encyclopaedia,* Vol. I. Chicago: The Howard Severance Company, 1901.

Dolphin, Lambert T. *Astrology, Occultism, and the Drug Culture.* Westchester, Illinois: Good News Publishers, 1970.

Edersheim, Alfred. *The Life and Times of Jesus, the Messiah.* Grand Rapids: Eerdmans, 1956.

Elwood, Roger. *Strange Things Are Happening.* Elgin, Illinois: David C. Cook, 1973.

Gasson, Raphael. *The Challenging Counterfeit.* Plainfield, New Jersey: Logus International, 1972.

Hough, Robert Ervin. *The Christian After Death.* Chicago: Moody Press, 1947.

Hoyt, Herman A. *The End Times.* Chicago: Moody Press, 1973.

Jamieson, R. "Divination." *The Popular and Critical Bible Encyclopaedia,* Vol. I. Chicago: The Howard Severance Company, 1901.

Joppie, A.S. *All About Angels.* Grand Rapids: Baker Book House, 1973.

Knight, Walker L. *The Weird World of the Occult.* Wheaton, Illinois: Tyndale Publishers, 1972.

Koch, Kurt E. *Between Christ and Satan.* Grand Rapids: Kregel Publications, 1962.

_____. *The Devil's Alphabet.* Grand Rapids: Kregel Publications, 1972.

Lawrence, E. A. "Spirit" *The Popular and Critical Bible Encyclopaedia,* Vol. II. Chicago: The Howard Severance Company, 1901.

Lindsey, Hal. *Satan Is Alive and Well on Planet Earth.* Grand Rapids: Zondervan, 1972.

Linton, John. *I Believe in Angels.* Grand Rapids: Eerdmans, 1952.

_____. *Concerning Infants in Heaven.* Grand Rapids: Eerdmans, 1949.

Lovett, C. S. *Dealing with the Devil.* Baldwin Park, California: Personal Christianity, 1967.

Marais, J. I. "Spirit." *International Standard Bible Encyclopaedia,* Vol. V. Grand Rapids: Eerdmans, 1939.

_____. "Soul." *International Standard Bible Encyclopaedia,* Vol. V. Grand Rapids: Eerdmans, 1939.

Maunder, E. W. "Astrology." *International Standard Bible Encyclopaedia,* Vol. I. Grand Rapids: Eerdmans, 1939.

McClain, Alva J. *Biblical Eschatology.* Unpublished Notes. Winona Lake, Indiana: Grace Theological Seminary.

Miller, C. Leslie. *All About Angels.* Glendale, California: G/L Publications, 1973.

Morgan, G. Campbell. *The Teaching of Christ.* New York: Revell, 1913.

_____. *The Gospel According to Matthew.* New York: Revell, 1929.

Needham, Mrs. George C. *Angels and Demons.* Chicago: Moody Press.

Newman, Joseph, Directing Editor. "The Religious Awakening in America." *U. S. News and World Report, Inc.* 1972.

Pache, Rene. *The Future Life.* Chicago: Moody Press, 1962.

Penn-Lewis, Mrs. *War On the Saints.* Leicester, England: The Excelsior Press, 1912.

Pember, C. H. *Earth's Earliest Ages.* New York: Revell.

Phillips, McCandlish. *The Bible, the Supernatural, and the Jews.* New York: The World Publishing Company, 1970.

Phillips, O. E. *Out of the Night.* Philadelphia: Hebrew Christian Fellowship, Inc., 1949.

Sauer, Erich. *The Dawn of World Redemption.* Grand Rapids: Eerdmans, 1952.

Strauss, Lehman. *The Doctrine of Man.* Findlay, Ohio: Dunham Publishing Company, 1959.

Strong, Augustus Hopkins. *Systematic Theology.* Philadelphia: Judson Press, 1906.

Trench, Richard C. *Notes on the Parables of Our Lord.* Westwood, New Jersey: Revell, 1953.

Unger, Merrill F. *Biblical Demonology.* Wheaton, Illinois: Scripture Press, 1972.

_____. *The Haunting of Bishop Pike.* Wheaton, Illinois: Tyndale House Publishers, 1971.

Whitcomb, John C., Jr. *The Early Earth.* Winona Lake, Indiana: BMH Books, and Grand Rapids: Baker Book House, 1972.

Winter, David. *Hereafter—What Happens After Death?* Wheaton, Illinois: The Christian Book Foundation Trust, 1973.

Wright, J. Stafford. *Christianity and the Occult.* Chicago: Moody Press, 1972.

_____. *Man in the Process of Time.* Grand Rapids: Eerdmans, 1956.